T0158722

A
CITY
IMAGINED

By the same author

Poetry

Sheltering Places
The Lundys Letter
Sunday School
Heart of Hearts
The Morning Train
Lake Geneva
Points West
Selected Poems
Mickey Finn's Air
The Last Peacock

Prose

Of War and War's Alarms
In Another World
Looking Through You
The Wrong Country
The Sound of the Shuttle

As editor

The Younger Irish Poets
Earth Voices Whispering
The Cambridge Companion to Irish Poets

GERALD DAWE

A
CITY
IMAGINED

Belfast Soulscapes

MERRION
PRESS

First published in 2021 by
Merrion Press
10 George's Street
Newbridge
Co. Kildare
Ireland
www.merrionpress.ie

9781785373930 (Cloth)
9781785373947 (Kindle)
9781785373954 (Epub)

A CIP catalogue record for this book is available from the
British Library.

Typeset in Sabon 11/15

Cover design: edit+ www.stuartcoughlan.com

Merrion Press is a member of Publishing Ireland.

For Conor Graham

CONTENTS

The author with Padraic Fiacc.
© Reproduced by kind permission of Bobbie Hanvey
Photographic Archives, Boston College.

PREFACE

When I was in my mid-60s, I came to the realisation that the stories handed down to me by my mother as a young lad in the 1950s in Belfast made me want to write. They emerged at any time and in any circumstance. An overheard strain of music on the radio would set her off; a look or smile from a fellow passenger on the bus; a rediscovered official document like a ration book from the Second World War; a piece of furniture in a shop window. They all brought recollection and history into the most fleeting of alignments, mostly unselfconsciously, or so I thought at the time. One morning not so long ago I caught myself absent-mindedly in the reflection of a mirror in our house in Dún Laoghaire. For a split second I was looking not at myself – a somewhat worn, bespectacled, middle-aged man – but the cast of my late mother was bizarrely present.

A second look and the impression had gone, along with the surprise. In the disorientation, I think I also encountered the extent to which the past is never really lost sight of but lives on in those stories we are told by our elders, and which we, in turn, make our own and hand on. Like guidelines. Points of reference. Hints about what the future might hold.

My mother had a very strong sense of family and its

past, even though it was not a simple or an easy story. Those bits of memory were carried like seeds in the wind from as far back as the 1850s, over a century before I first heard them. Tales about my great-grandmother in India, with her improvident military father. Or her subsequent life in Edwardian Belfast; the family's never-ending movement out of the city to England, or Canada, or the United States, and always the inevitable return to Belfast. The city was like a magnetic pull.

These fragments of stories were more often than not connected to the houses my mother lived in and there were many of them. Temporary homes for the early part of her life, captured in photographs with captions handwritten on the back. 'Snowbound in Toronto'. This would have been in the 1920s. 'Visiting the Zoo': this, London in the 1930s. 'Gaga' – the family name for my great-grandfather – 'in the garden at Park Avenue', maybe a little later, in Hendon. Asleep as it happens, in his three-piece suit. Another photo has him stretching for a bottle of beer. It has to be summer, just before the war. Later, in the 1960s, I'd be lolling about that garden too. Over in London for a wedding, no doubt.

In her retelling details, the houses she lived in took on a momentary presence in profile, a hinted-at life, but none had as much imaginative draw for my mother as the house in Duncairn Gardens off the Antrim Road in north Belfast where she grew up, returned briefly to during the war and left again to marry. The house stood at the top of the Gardens.

A somewhat sombre-looking, even foreboding, high terraced house, with its curtains neatly drawn. It no longer exists and the Gardens themselves are long gone. I recall the bus ambling along the Antrim Road and her turning her head slightly in the direction of the old house when I was a young boy heading into town on Saturday mornings to accompany her shopping. It was obvious that the house, where she and her brother had lived with their mother, had etched itself upon her mind. When it was sold, the family moved about a mile away in the same district and settled in a smaller version of the same style of house.

A house of women it was, too. Great-grandmother, she of the Indian experience, her daughter, my grand-mother, my mother and my sister, until I came along and we moved to a newly built estate of houses tucked beside a golf course and called 'Downview' because, across the lough, County Down rolled away.

And though those years in Downview eventually became unhappy ones for my mother and we moved once more, back to my grandmother's house, there was a vague sense of the countryside about our time there in the 1950s. Visiting her friends in the old red-brick avenues must have reminded her of a previous life, so by the time she had moved once again, this time to the east of the city, these places were receding and losing their reality as homes. It was only a matter of a generation before the Downview estate was demolished and new-styled condominiums went up in their place. As one home joined another in her memory bank, the past would survive in a chair or a mirror which had remained from a century before, when they all started on their travels.

In the early 1980s, I was sitting in a room in what was a forgotten part of the west of Ireland, a town battered around between pillar and post – a town, to all intents and purposes, no longer sure what to make of itself. Around me were my wife, son, daughter and in-laws. The talk was hectic, it being some time since we had visited my mother-in-law, her sister and her brother, all of whom were in their 80s.

The gathering was in the small living room that looked onto a main road. The talk drifted unpredictably from one thing to another, with the past like a rudder, shifting us this way and that. Of Michael Collins and who had killed him; of England during 'the war', where my aunt had worked as a district nurse; of weever fish, whose reactive prongs can poison and numb an arm for months; of life in gaol during the War of Independence; of a returned distant relative and his family; of recent deaths and how they had stripped the town of more of the old inhabitants – people who had experienced Ireland's history at first hand, participated in some of it, but, for the rest of their time, were outside and resigned, their feeling for history and politics determined by that place.

I was sitting in the room listening and, after a while, I turned on the radio and heard someone discuss 'Poetry and Modern Society'. The difference was immediate. With the room so full of talk – details of history, fragments of politics, of de Valera's head looking like that of an Indian's, of the weather and how it was changing – the sheer cacophonous energy was of many voices telling their own story and all seeking to be heard. And here on the radio was one voice, calm and controlled, being listened to, presumably with interest, in various homes, flats and rooms throughout the country.

The contrast was stark and severe, but it portrayed the kind of forces with which a poet must deal. Maybe not at the level of an individual poem, a specific image or scene, but in the back room of the imagination, where poems are first made and developed, that clambering-for-expression with its own vitality and insistence exerts for me a special influence on what a poet writes.

This influence leads in two directions at the same time – away from the gaggle and Babel's tower of living, but also towards it, trying to hold those elements of it with which one can cope. Rarely is there a satisfactory balance. The poet is confined to only a part of speech and tries to make a poem that is entire and complete, unlike life, where failure, defeat, injustice and pain so often interrupt and snatch freedom away. This is not to suggest that poets and poetry must necessarily speak as if success, triumph, equality, hope and love were abandoned concepts. But I do not want to sound either like an evangelist. Hope, love, injustice are just words, abstractions in the same way that the word 'language' is when related to the scene I have just described. I think, too, of another scene.

It is the late 1950s in the front room of that red-bricked house in a terraced row of seven houses, wedged between Belfast's Cave Hill and the Lough: a world of small gardens, minute backyards; a dark scullery and two flights of creaking stairs that lead past, like a look-out post, the bathroom. The mock stained-glass spangling light on the landing with two bedrooms, their fireplaces blocked, huge wardrobes and uncertain windows and, at the top of the house, my own den, with its slanting ceilings, the piles of family mementoes and sheet music stashed in the corner, and the chimney alive with sparrows.

In the front room, a large mirror leans above the mantelpiece before which a baize card table is placed; to its right a closed Steinway piano, and to the left a bay window basking in the last of the late-afternoon light. You can hear, just about, the tock of a grandfather clock on the landing. Also, my grandmother's voice instructing a young girl from the district how to recite a poem 'properly'. It is Wednesday: elocution class with Ethel, light-opera singer, shop assistant, belle, who has in front of her *Palgrave's Golden Treasury* opened at 'The Daffodils':

> I wandered lonely as a cloud
> That floats on high o'er vales and hills,
> When all at once I saw a crowd,
> A host, of golden daffodils;
> Beside the lake, beneath the trees,
> Fluttering and dancing in the breeze.

The girl pupil, one of many, speaks the words with urgent feeling, the stresses and inflections in keeping with convention. The girl watches her own mouth in the mirror as Ethel mouths the syllables in a prompting mime. For Ethel, it is a love and a profession. She taps out the rhythm like a conductor. The poem sings in a controlled and articulate manner. It has been mastered and the girl, in a pretty dress, will win a little cup and go into the world confident of the way she speaks, vowels like balloons, the head swaying ever so slightly. Until, probably, marriage, and the certain slow reclaiming of her own accent from that sophisticated gloss, which maybe did not *really* help her 'get on' in the world after all.

This scene, which I witnessed as a small boy in my grandmother's house, opening doors to the hopeful and the ambitious, comes to my mind when I think about the poetic craft. And here, too, both scenes play across each other – the helter-skelter of impressions; the mannered poise; the fragments and figments of history; the cultivated grace; the 'nationalist' west; the 'unionist' north-east; each entailing its own hurt and insecurities, pride and prejudice, and how these are expressed differently. Is this where the poet comes in, uncalled for, but there all the same, summarising the complexity as best he or she can, discerning what is humanly possible?

The greatest influence on a writer is the past, and its relevance is pervasive in what follows and is the source on which this short book is based. Often it is only when that past is unearthed that a poet begins to make sense of his or her imaginings. Somehow the recovery of the world of the past not only helps a poet show what makes up the world, but also helps turn it into a more 'liveable' place in the here and now. In this sense, a poet is strictly 'anti-nostalgic'. In my own case, most of my poems are about this process. It is the voices of mood and the objective turn of event which fascinate me, how they live in the memory, unsettling, probing, and making us think and feel in certain ways.

A City Imagined: Belfast Soulscapes opens in one of the houses I return to here and takes in the outlines of my own life as I started to understand the city in which I was born, before embracing some of the local writers, overwhelmingly male as is obvious from what follows, whose early work had such an influential part in nudging me in the direction of writing – poets, in the main, whose first books were read with the enthusiasm of a very young man beguiled by the language and the music of poetry.

Gerald Dawe
Dún Laoghaire & Belfast
July 2021

ONE

So, it began next door, in the house I moved to as a young boy in the Belfast of the 1950s. That terraced row comprised fairly typical late Victorian, not particularly graceful, houses. What made the neighbourhood important were the people who lived there. Next door there was an Austrian woman who had fallen in love with a dashing young Northern Irish soldier stationed in Vienna at the end of the Second World War. She was an incredibly tall woman who 'dressed up'; she bred pedigree poodles and spoke with a very pronounced 'foreign' accent. Next door to this lady and her extremely quiet, civil servant husband, was a large family with whom I became very friendly; indeed, at one stage of my boyhood, I was almost a foster son of this family. They were a Catholic family, unlike my own, and I loved being with them. My mother did not mind my disappearing for long stretches of the day, nor did my grandmother with whom we lived, and during the 1950s and 1960s this little patch of Belfast – that terrace, the encircling avenues, main roads, that district – was my home. I knew it, as we say, like the back of my hand.

I count myself lucky to have been brought up in that particular place and time, because from my boyhood, without actually knowing it then, I was experiencing difference; cultural diversity as we would say now. The Catholic family became very much a part of our life. So, too, did the Austrian lady, who fascinated me with her domestic rituals of thick rich coffee in small cups, the fancy pastries, and her strange mix of formality and vulnerability. A little later, in the mid-1960s, I also became very friendly with several Jewish families who lived in our immediate district. That cultural mix was healthy: there was a synagogue, a delicatessen, and a hairstylist – all part of the local fabric; it freed up the mind, maybe not in contemporaneous time, but afterwards, later on. It is important to state this as bluntly as possible, given what we now know was to happen in Belfast by the late 1960s and early 1970s, as the city turned into a bloody site of sectarian warfare and a struggle for political (and cultural) supremacy and retribution. Indeed, the particular area of north Belfast which I am describing became one of the most bitter interface areas of sectarian conflict, with Protestant families accusing Catholic families of seeking to 'ethnically cleanse' them from the area.

Catholic families, on the other hand, countered with accusations of constant sectarian attacks from loyalist gangs, all fed by generations of suspicion and institutional hostility from both church and state to integrated education.

The history of Belfast since its emergence as an industrial city in the 1840s was very much wrapped up with the economic destiny of Britain. The city drew into its constricted low-lying basin hundreds of thousands of unskilled and skilled workers from the rural Irish hinterlands, from Scotland and from England. With the foundation of the Irish Free State in 1922 and the partition of Ireland, the substantial Catholic minority remaining inside the new Northern Irish 'Protestant' state felt isolated and marooned within a hostile political culture. The failure to seriously integrate that Catholic minority ultimately led to the eruption of the 'Troubles', which left thousands dead and countless thousands maimed both physically and psychologically, primarily in Northern Ireland, but also in the Republic, in Britain and in Continental Europe. The lesson is obvious here for our globalised world of the twenty-first century. Against this bloody backdrop, the cultural mix that I mentioned as being a part of my own upbringing in Belfast has been largely destroyed. In its place emerged 'no-go' areas that eventually mutated into a patchwork landscape of exclusionist districts, either Protestant or Catholic, loyalist or nationalist, ring-fenced against each other with the grotesquely named Peace Lines demarcating a divided city, which in turn reflected a divided province. Today Northern Ireland lives in a cultural flux, with groups of its people living their lives in a constantly contested battle of flags and emblems, mutually excluding one another, either physically or symbolically. It is a war of words now as much as anything else.

One can in part see the Northern Ireland situation, or the Belfast situation, as a political analogue to what was to happen throughout Eastern Europe by the time the communist states crumbled and the refrigerated ethnic tensions resurfaced without any powerful civic intervention and mediation. Paramilitary or para-political forces on the ground parcelled up parts of Belfast as the overarching political system stalled. The fallout, in terms of law and order, drug problems, localised power struggles, political patronage and favour, is the evening news bulletins to this very day. Northern Ireland is going through the latest protracted attempt to restore some form of accountable democracy to a people who still do not know how to civically imagine and share what each other has actually been through during the past thirty years. Behind the parliamentary language of compromise and mutual understanding there is a huge gulf of mistrust and ignorance, upon which the bigots and violence junkies still prey. It is a minuscule version of what takes place when multicultural democratic governments do not seriously tackle the ideological and economic impulses of fundamentalism. For much of this intense local political gamesmanship has an obvious, direct and critical bearing upon the template of possibilities which in this part of the world we call 'Europe'.

I was schooled in British history; to most of my generation the Second World War was part of our psychic and social landscape whether we liked it or not. The public figures of that time, the names of battles, the sense of war and destruction in countries and cities, the names of which we heard in school, on television and in film, filled up my mind and my imagination. Yet it was a 'Europe' in fundamental ways distant. It started to take on a much more personal meaning when in the mid-1960s I saw a photograph in *The Observer* (commemorating the beginning of the war) of a young Jewish boy being rounded up by the Gestapo, his arms raised, his large cap seeming too large for his frightened face. Somewhat later, I followed with fascination developments in (as it then was) Czechoslovakia and wrote a poem in homage to Jan Palach, the young student who set himself on fire in Wenceslas Square in Prague in protest at the Soviet invasion and the ensuing closure of the borders between Czechoslovakia and the outside world. Many years later I met a Czech émigré on a family holiday in Santorini. His sense of where he came from and what he belonged to exposed my own frail knowledge of where this place 'Europe' actually was and is, while the map he drew on a napkin is embossed forever in my mind.

I also started to probe my own family background and discovered that on one side of the family, my mother's side, we had been refugees (with the name Chartres) who arrived in Ireland during the persecution of the Huguenots in France, while my maternal great-grandmother carried the surname Quartz. Alongside this mixture there were, on my maternal grandfather's side, well-established roots in Fermanagh in the north-west of Ireland, and my own (estranged) father was born in London but had connections with the England–Wales border. This amounted to a kind of cultural dispensation, a cultural coding. So, when I started to think about what 'European' identity meant, it occurred to me that many share, possibly without even knowing it, a multicultural familial past and that this will become increasingly common if present patterns of migration continue throughout Europe.

None of this consciousness would have come through formal schooling. It is random and unstructured, related more to chance – an Austrian neighbour next door – as much as genealogy. But probe ever so lightly into most families and one will find the variable figure, the different strain, influence or background. The problem is when this difference is locked away, either literally or metaphorically, in the (political, economic or cultural) interests of one exclusive dominant identity: the prison of fundamentalism. What happens then can become shocking beyond belief, as the Second World War demonstrated and as the end of the twentieth century showed in Bosnia, Kosovo and elsewhere; horrifying measures of ethnic cleansing just do not disappear. Now much enlarged and enlarging, Europe is becoming smaller than it ever was before. A matter of three or four hours could take me from my front door in Dublin to Belgrade, or what was once the cauldron of Kosovo.

The proximity is important because we have to imagine a time when the reconstructed democracies of former Yugoslavia, Albania and Romania become a truly functioning and permanent part of Europe, alongside Poland, Slovenia and the Czech and Slovak Republics. And what about the powder keg that Turkey is becoming – a great, culturally rich society that edges at times to racist, nationalist and religious extremism?

Europe can be an extraordinary federation, as thousands of people cross borders and make new lives for themselves in other parts of the continent, bringing with them their different histories, customs, beliefs and cultures. How we adjust to these changes under the pressure of deepening economic difficulties is (as Brexit has shown) *the* crucial defining test of political will in the twenty-first century. But there remains the critical template of possibility – of a European identity embracing all Europe, not just its western flank, but its central and middle core and eastern periphery. No nation (super or otherwise) will ever be called 'Europe' and maybe its meaning resides in that very fact – of potentiality, ideal and dream. People will discover other places, not only on a couple of weeks' holiday but as a reimagining of all our histories. A new kind of inclusive historical consciousness can take root, if we prepare the ground for such a transformation in terms of mass education based upon mutual respect and the honouring of difference; not as threat but as human richness.

In the final year of the last century, I was rereading 'Autumn Journal', Louis MacNeice's great poem, written in 1938. The poem, which is in twenty-four cantos, contains in its final canto the lines 'Let us dream it now/And pray for a possible land' – lines that have always haunted me, coming as they did just before the deluge of the Second World War. Sitting on the balcony of a hotel room, I wrote 'Summer Journal' as a song to innocence and hope, and a prelude to the new century, shadowed by the terrible scenes of the war happening in the room next door, on our television screen:

Summer Journal
for Brendan Kennelly

1
Through the porthole of a window
The blue muggy night is perforated
With the sound of foghorns.
Dogs answer each other back
And then it thunders again with spectacular effect.
The girls are sleeping in the cool apartment;
Shadows like planes cast over the lawn.
I'm in two minds between *Tender is the Night*
And the TV's mute hectic images
Which flash worldwide the breaking news
Of a hillside trek and scorched villages,
The bedecked impromptu briefing.

2
The ignominious beetle covers oceans of sand
But the man or woman who drifts
Into the sky, paragliding over our prone bodies –
Family groups setting up makeshift home,
Couples in their prime and past their prime,
The odd one alone stretched under the sun
Where all are vulnerable, torn this way
And that, naked, flat, in repose from
The everyday, at sixes and sevens –
Is trussed and hooked to the speeding boat
And, cradled like a baby, looks down
Upon us all with far-seeing love and pity.

3

Palm doves and swallows in the apricot
And oleander, the cacophony
Of high season; poolside, *Mitteleuropa*
Tans and in silence observes a galleon
Take up the full of the bay.
The rosé goes down like mother's milk;
It's near ninety, best head for cover;
In the shade local dance music
Beats through the scratchy airwaves
To you on whichever island you stand:
'*Let us dream it now,*
and pray for a possible land.'

TWO

The two who called to our front door are probably into their 70s by now. My mother was expecting the call, but when the doorbell rang we were both still taken a little by surprise.

Could she allow me to join a band? I would be well looked after. *I need a black polo neck and dark trousers. There'd be rehearsals after Scouts, and occasional weekends.* She agreed and thus began my very brief career as a singer in a 'rock' band. It probably didn't last more than six months and I played, I think, about three times on stage 'live', so to speak. Two or three cover songs of 'Gloria' (what else?), The Kinks' 'All Day and All of the Night' and 'Let's Spend the Night Together' by The Rolling Stones. The rest of the set was instrumentals – 'Apache' and 'Wipe Out' – which showed how good our drummer was. The band, The Trolls, was a four-piece outfit consisting of bass player (Georgie), lead guitarist (Eric), drummer (Roger) and singer (yours truly). There may have been a further fifth member, but that's how I recall it, fifty years on. Our practice sessions took place in a house on the Cave Hill Road and in the Scout hall of the 78th Duncairn troop, down a laneway that ran parallel to Glandore Avenue and in behind a row of shops (at one time), including a Jewish hairdresser and delicatessen, on the Antrim Road.

The only 'real' memory I have of actually singing was in a talent competition in a hotel on the main street in Bangor. To liven things up, I had maracas, which I shook while moving about on stage. The previous night a showband (The Royal, I think) had inadvertently split one of the timbers on stage, in which my prancing foot momentarily stuck, taking a little of the polish off my performance, if one can call it that. Most things were made up as we went along, except for the order of songs (of which there were only a very limited number); what happened in between and during was unrehearsed, moveable. Anyway, we came in second on the 'Applause Meter' – a simple device that was manually worked according to the volume of applause the judge interpreted as greeting on stage each of the representatives from the various performers and 'acts'. I was the mascot that night in Bangor and I can still remember my sense of disbelief as I watched the judge work a pedal as the applause meter flashed into action like a fairground gadget and then fell back to zero as he took his inspired foot off the pedal! 'Second' wasn't so bad after all; indeed things could have been worse.

In the van back to Belfast, we inadvertently parked for a pit stop on the crest of a hill and luckily no one stepped out of the back as the unprotected siding gave onto a severe drop of a couple of hundred feet down an embankment. That would have been a more serious dint to our pride.

Through the band I met a few other lads, slightly older than my fifteen years in 1967, many of whom were, like me, in the scouts. The troop was culturally mixed, and friends I made there came from Protestant and Jewish backgrounds in the lower- and middle-class neighbourhoods of north Belfast. My own family had lived in the area since the turn of the nineteenth century and had, in the form of my mother's grandparents, prospered, living in a large, terraced house at the top of Duncairn Gardens (since demolished). Later, my grandmother (with whom my mother, sister and I lived), having returned from Canada and London, settled with her, by then, widowed mother literally around the corner from the Scout Hall off the Antrim Road.

This was 'my' part of Belfast from the mid-1950s to the late 1960s. Through the landscape, streets, histories, customs and lifestyle of that mixed and varied mini-society, I discovered myself and ultimately the complex meaning of Northern Irish society.

But back to The Trolls. I think it was through the band that I joined, as a 15-year-old, the PPU (Peace Pledge Union), took in the last hurrah of the CND (Campaign for Nuclear Disarmament), first came in contact with NICPV (the Northern Ireland Campaign for Peace in Vietnam), attended occasional 'fast' sessions outside the City Hall, handing out leaflets, and, on Sunday nights, sat in 'Heaven', the white church at the side of the City Hall, drinking tea and chatting up girls.

Central to much of this campaigning was Orange-field Boys School, in east Belfast, where daily I bussed across from my northside home, along with significant numbers of other students from all over Belfast: Stranmillis, Ballygomartin, Malone, as well as its immediate hinterland of Castlereagh, Beersbridge, Newtownards and Braniel roads. The school had a reputation for liberal and progressive educational policies and was noted for the quality of its teaching staff, working under the visionary headmaster John Malone, including 'Dai' Francis, Jonathan Bardon, Davy Hammond, the Sinnerton brothers and Sam McCready, who set in motion the Lyric Youth Theatre which produced out of Orangefield a generation of talented actors and others involved in the radio, television, theatre and film worlds.

The other important figure in those mid-1960s days was Terri Hooley, whom I had briefly met in a very small office at the top of a rickety stairway in a building in High Street. The Bahá'í faith was in an office below him. From here Terri sent out his willing troops to advise the good people of Belfast about the inequities of Vietnam. We even had a Vietnamese flag on display, although on one occasion I recall, when a counter-demonstration took place outside the City Hall involving some Protestant fundamentalists, they took exception to the flag and one of their number lifted it from its holder, denouncing us as communists and the devil knows what. He had not, however, reckoned on the swift and physical retaliation of a somewhat inebriated sailor who had temporarily taken us under his wing, applauding whatever he could make out from the mashed exhortations being shouted down our loudspeaker. A nifty head-butt sprawled the thin-faced, previously ecstatic, now ashen-faced, preacher, and our flag was promptly restored to its rightful place. Our proselytising competitor slipped farther along the City Hall railings to where the flower-sellers were packing up for the day.

Saturday late afternoons were like that. Across the road somewhat later, in maybe 1968, a young man selling the *Free Citizen* was goaded and prodded and finally smacked by three or four men who were far from happy with his shouts of complaint against the Northern state. I can still hear his brave young voice, frightened yet unbowed, at the corner of Gilpin's in Royal Avenue, and the women who surrounded him and patted him and helped him back to his feet.

Out of these disparate little groups of 1960s' hopes and fears, experiments and fascinations, from the periphery of which I observed with keen interest, the social life of Belfast changed and, from the viewpoint of the young, tuned into the big world of British and, particularly, American popular culture and politics. My own interest in politics ebbed and flowed, and because of this vacillation I never really stuck at any one thing for any length of time. The popular culture was defining and probably at its peak on both radio and television, as well as producing some of the best in 'pop' music. When The Trolls disappeared, and the scouts, folk music came into the frame with real-life sessions scattered around the city centre in pubs and clubs and a couple of private homes, but this was towards the end of the 1960s, just before the curtain fell and the 'Troubles' took over all our lives. There was a brief period of immense freedom when Belfast, including the north of the city, saw young men and women from all kinds of religious backgrounds (and none) mixing at parties when parents were away, after school in coffee bars in town, outside shops on the Antrim Road, criss-crossing town for a date, going to the 'flicks' and, of course, the endless listening to music and dancing, forever dancing. For the music scene in Belfast was *the* scene.

Whatever happened in the front rooms, drawing rooms, back bedrooms and attics of the houses where all these young men and women gathered – dressed in the various fashions of the time, reading the same rock magazines, buying the same albums – the idea that in five or six years their lives would be ruled by sectarian overlords, paramilitary courts, or that political passions would lead some of their number to maim and murder fellow citizens, was simply beyond belief. It still catches me out, I have to say.

The vortex of the 'Troubles', which was building up under the surface of Belfast life at that time, was built on powerful resentments and generations of injustice and mistrust. We were like tightrope walkers who kept looking forward; we never looked back. If the world was at fault it was Vietnam, the Bomb, but what this city of Belfast was, was home, girls, music, clothes, Bangor, Portrush, the sea, the sand. The pubs: Kelly's Cellars, The Olde House, The Scrumpy Rooms, The Fiddler's. Sitting upstairs in the Queen's Arcade pub and looking down on a Saturday afternoon as shoppers milled about and a war veteran mouthed into his harmonica looking for a few pennies. Sammy Houston's, The Maritime, Inst, the Floral Hall. Dances; dancing galore. And Top of the Pops; Ready, Steady, Go; 6.5 Special; Play for Today. And all those great bands playing the Ulster Hall. You name it. They all played there. Not unionism or nationalism. Not history. Not 1690. Not 1916. What was all that about? It was not wilful blindness so much as youthful ignorance and maybe an instinctive desire not to be cowed by the past.

When I was about 15, someone suggested I should get a summer job. Through a school friend I ended up as a plasterer's mate in Carrickfergus, stripping down the interior of a laundromat so that the plasterer could begin the proper work of smoothing and sweeping across the walls. It was a badge of honour to return home dust-capped and tired rather than the somewhat dissolute being of rising late and reading into the wee hours.

That job didn't last very long, so my memory tells me anyway. The next 'real job' was at a large petrol station on the Antrim Road as a car-washer. It was an experience which I should best forget. Nit-picking car owners – 'You missed the hubcaps'; 'What about the front light on the left?' – remain like burrs in the mind alongside the bright, brilliant cast of sunlight sparking off the white rooftops during a Belfast high summer. We wore 'shades' and looked a little like the kids in *West Side Story* in our denims, T-shirts and basketball boots. But the first real challenge came a few years later and it changed the way I thought about things.

It was Christmas 1969 and I was a temporary postman. I wore a little armband with a crown on it and my 'route', bulging bag slung over my shoulder, contained letters and cards from all over the world, which I delivered to rows of terraced homes throughout what would become known as the 'west' of the city. I'd have my set of pigeonholes to fill out, street by street, number by number, and bind the letters up into bundles with strong rubber bands. In the sorting office, music kept us going. Lots of men standing before their wooden walls of boxes; the experienced ones could talk and work at the same time. Or sing. It was a sight to behold. One of the songs we would sing along to was Neil Diamond's 'Sweet Caroline', or the mind-numbing 'Sugar, Sugar' by The Archies. Things, however, got serious when Elvis, a role model for my more senior contemporaries, came over the radio with 'Suspicious Minds'; the entire floor, present writer included, joined in the chorus. And unless my recollection deceives me, I can also see those wonderful Belfast postmen making dance moves by their boxes.

It could be cold on the streets, really cold. Dogs roamed with abandon. In certain districts the crown badge had on occasion to be inverted – a recommendation I accepted without any thought – and it wasn't unusual to have a following of kids like the Pied Piper. My first term as a temporary postman shook me out of my complacency about some of the housing conditions in this pre-Troubles Belfast, where poverty was etched in the very fabric of some houses and in some of the welcoming faces that greeted the delivery of a small parcel or letter.

On one street, I vividly recall a corner house which had obviously once been a shop. The entrance was dark and dingy as I entered, seeking someone to sign for the parcel I had. The barren rooms led towards a bare stairway and, as I called out, the owner shouted down for me to come up and he'd sign for the present. His living quarters were like something out of Dickensian London.

My life as a postman lasted only a couple of seasons, taking me into well-paid overtime in my final tour of office as an undergraduate working one summer and one final snow-filled Christmas. We assembled that Christmas Eve in an ebullient public house. I was the kid on the block swigging down pints of what was then known as 'Single' Guinness (yes, there was also 'Double' and the apocryphal 'Treble'). In that smoke-filled, non-stop-talking, magical bar – long since gone – with its mahogany tables, high ceilings, original Victorian fittings, stained-glass windows and aproned barmen, I felt as if I had finally made something of myself.

Calling in with a friend to a house at the junction of the Antrim Road and Duncairn Gardens to meet up with our girls of the time, we were invited into a fine house of comfortable, welcoming proportions. As we stood momentarily in the hallway of that typical Belfast Victorian home, a large painting of Our Lord, with votive lamp underneath it, glowed in the dusk of early evening and rhythmic sounds came out from the pantry. We exchanged perplexed glances, hunched shoulders and in a moment our girls appeared, radiant in their mini-skirts, blouses and dancing shoes after reciting the rosary, and we made the bus, heading straight for town and Betty Staffs or the Jazz Club. On Saturday nights, I would call for my friend Lou and wait for his evening supper and prayers to be complete before we'd head off; once or twice joining in with yarmulke on, not having the faintest clue what was happening. We might collect on the way Ken, whose father had fought as a rear-gunner in the big aerial battles of the Second World War, and walk past the imposing Presbyterian Church at the corner of Skegoneill and the Antrim Road towards Somerton or Downview or back through Glandore, past so many different homes, to meet up with someone else – Protestants and Catholics and Jews; lapsed this and that. Gospel halls, Saved by the Blood of the Lamb. A synagogue. A British Legion hall. A Catholic convent girls' school. A Protestant secondary school. It just went on and on. Grammar school, corner shop, lounge bar, hotel, gardens, entries, until we hopped another bus and were in town by 7.30 p.m. And all over the city the same thing was happening. Young men and women in their teens and early 20s were thinking about Saturday night, not Monday morning or Sunday service. A vibrant life spread throughout that generation in 1967 and maybe there was an awareness that something new was breaking through and that we didn't need to worry or complain about 'where' you were 'from', what school you went to, in order to sort and file under Protestant, Catholic, Jew, dissenter, unionist, nationalist, orange, green … I don't think it mattered then, not to us. Later, unquestionably; but not then, no. We had a ball, no matter what anyone says.

The chance was briefly in the air. As we know, at the close of the 1960s Belfast fell into a time warp; almost half a century later it looks like it just might, with a bit of luck, be back on track again.

THREE

I was in Dublin for the first time in 1967, aged 15 going on 16. David Craig, an enterprising art teacher at Orangefield, took a small group of his Art History class to an exhibition of modern painting at the Royal Dublin Society, preceded by a visit to the National Museum for an exhibition of ancient Celtic art. Or it could have been the other way around since it is quite some time ago and I can't recall the train journey to Dublin. What I do remember is stepping into Connolly Station with the thrill of knowing that we were in Dublin. For young Belfast Protestants in the mid-1960s such a journey would have been relatively rare. One image surfaces, though, of seeing kids sitting on the steps to the railway station playing cards and begging. And, unless I'm imagining it, they had no jumpers or socks on. How we got to and from the RDS and the National Museum has also passed me by in the intervening years. ROSC '67, the catalogue of which I have open in front of me, exploded in my mind. Beyond all the paintings and sculptures on display, there was not one in particular which shook me, although the ectoplasmic 'Soft Skoob' sculpture was disturbingly alive. It was the cumulative effect of so much modern art in the one place that did it. Dubuffet, Bacon, de Kooning, Lichtenstein, Nicholson,

Picasso, Rauschenberg, Vasarely and the intriguing sign language of Miró turned the exhibition into a 'poetry of vision' which appealed so much to the inchoate young man I then was.

The Celtic exhibition – exquisite artefacts of an ancient culture – encased in the display cabinets, shaped and preserved in the contemporary Ireland of the 1960s, did not have quite the same effect at all. Its sheer beauty was remote. The museum, the library, Kildare Street, Leinster House, those national institutions just evaporated into the smoggy Dublin air. So I've been thinking about that trip and what, if any, meaning can be drawn from it as I come to terms with what happened to both cities, Belfast and Dublin, after 1967: the years of the 'Troubles'. Something about that trip keeps coming back to me as a kind of litmus test or a threshold experience. Belfast and Dublin have always had an interesting family association in both pre- and post-Partition Ireland. If historically Dublin was 'English' and Belfast 'British', underneath there has been a mutual understanding amongst the citizens of both cities.

Whatever about the political divisions and ignorant sectarian taunts and rants of individuals and groups, Dublin has enjoyed a special resonance to most free-thinking Belfast people. In recent years this attitude has been liberated from a sometime patronising belief that Belfast was 'of course' greater than the Dublin of the past, a belief in no way mean-spirited but based more on the inherited assumptions of Belfast's retaining its Britishness, spanning through the global network of imperial industrialisation during the late nineteenth and twentieth centuries. Dublin was seen as a remarkable, exciting city on the sidelines. All this has, of course, changed completely and Belfast has now to find a new identity for itself; new in many ways.

The post-industrial twenty-first century means that those colossal industrial roots to the city no longer count except as heritage. The post-'Troubles' city has also to cope with that violent legacy and the manner in which it retains a limited life in some of the flash-point areas. In contrast, Dublin from the late 1980s and early 1990s took off, unencumbered by the past. The connections with Europe, the loosening of the grip and gripe of old pieties – if not the major commercial ties – as regards England, certainly freed up a brash (and at times highly suspect) entrepreneurial spirit whose eagerness to do things was American but whose cultural frame of reference was European.

The scale of cultural prestige had been generally tipped towards Dublin, with Belfast seen as much more interested in 'business'. Given the change in fortunes in recent times, it goes to show just how vulnerable and variable these kinds of stereotypes can be.

In the 1950s and 1960s fleets of buses parked around Belfast's City Hall (on Thursdays was it?), having deposited hundreds of Dublin (and other southern) shoppers in the city centre. That trade has probably been reversed as the sense of weekend Dublin, shopping along with a good time in Temple Bar, lures the young and not so young to Dublin in their droves. In defiance of the savage brutalities of the past and of the attacks on that rail link by various backward republican and loyalist groups, what has survived the thirty years of the 'Troubles' is a connectedness which presents itself popularly as commercial ('great shopping') but actually means something else; something more. I think it has a lot to do with power and the common, historical exercise of power, even when that very exercise was in Belfast's case removed for almost a quarter of a century.

The use and idea of civic power and authority is a habit, or else it has to be learned. In Belfast's case, it is a question of stretching the franchise and unlearning some very bad, undemocratic practices. In Dublin, even in the dismal days of economic stagnation and social malfunction (such as the influence of the Roman Catholic Church), there has been a cosmopolitan sense of self-worth and cultural importance. As with other capitals, both cities looked over their shoulders to the city-state of London. Belfast was possibly marginally better placed to absorb other economic ties with, for instance, Liverpool and Glasgow. But by the 1990s and the new century, Dublin had almost convinced itself that it *was* London, or was that the other way around? Either way, a certain kind of cultural chutzpah ran the risk of turning hype into self-deluding chauvinism, something we continued to pay for in the grim austerity aftermath to the Celtic Tiger.

Which has taken me some way from that journey those boys made in 1967 heading down to Dublin from Belfast. It was not across any earth-shatteringly alien terrain, but it was to a different imagined place. I had seen some photographs of my glamorous grandmother and her dapper boyfriend of the time walking breezily through Dublin's O'Connell Street just after the Second World War. Dublin was connected in my mind at least with flamboyance and the risqué. By the late 1960s and early 1970s, I was smoking Carrolls and Major cigarettes and reading *The Irish Times* and *The Irish Press*, judiciously folded so that their mastheads could not be readily identified on the bus to the flat I temporarily shared in a loyalist east Belfast estate. But more to the point, Dublin was identified as an artistic place, which had exposed those boys to an abundance of paintings and sculptures, modern and contemporary artists, the likes of which were unavailable in snobbish, insulated Belfast, where 'Art' was more often than not seen as a best-kept secret.

That trip also posed, without my thinking about it at the time, the synchronicity of 'ancient' and 'modern' and of how everything exists in the same time frame of the here and now. The trouble is when the young are exposed to only one form of fundamental cultural identity and are told to believe that it – whatever 'it' is – is the *only* important self-defining identity available and worthwhile, and that anything else is foreign and lesser, to be mocked or ridiculed. This is what effectively happened over the next three decades as competing political ideologies in Belfast prescribed their own way of seeing things from the point of view of 'their' own people, their own 'community'. Are there young students from other state schools taking field trips to 'events' similar to ROSC '67? I hope so, but I don't know. The dominant culture which underpins contemporary lifestyle obsession drains much of the surprise from distance and difference, and supplants it with an ersatz hedonistic exhaustion; 'cool' exhaustion equals consumerist chic.

Maybe in the mid-1960s we were lucky to make the break when we did, so that we could see what the immediate parameters were – of home and family, neighbourhood and city. That trip to Dublin was as subtly subversive and potent an experience as any similar journey I have since taken. But maybe the 15- and 16-year-olds today are indeed travelling to the heartlands of European history, the battlefields, the Holocaust sites, the world-renowned art museums, the archaeological routes throughout Britain and the continent and farther afield. Maybe they are surfing the virtual realities on the Internet, impatient with next door, down the road, over the border: rapid options at the push of a button; synchronicity at speed, the truly imaginary museum? I don't know. Entangled, competitive histories, proximity and difference are valuable things to experience. Cultural exchange – a rather po-faced term – might as well start at home because we all have to live there, sometime or other.

FOUR

Several Northern writers mean a great deal to me. They were very influential, indeed instrumental, in shaping my early years. I think I'm not overstating it to say that without their example when I was starting off, I probably would have run out of steam and turned my mind to something else. They are not the sole voices I listened to in the mid- to late 1960s, but what makes them important to me is that they demonstrated that it was possible to come from Belfast and write about the place without condescension, or apology, or having to look over your shoulder at what was expected of you. In a way these different male voices proved at the time one simple if elusive truth, that Belfast possessed its own mysteries and landscape and ways of being which, with the right amount of luck and commitment, could produce writing of the first rank. I discovered Belfast through these writers and, in time, their example would lead me to write about the city in which I had grown up.

The irony is that, in the fifty or so years that separates the early beginnings in the writing careers of poets such as Seamus Heaney, Derek Mahon and Michael Longley (as well as the breakthrough novels of Brian Moore, Van Morrison's album *Astral Weeks* and Padraic Fiacc's first major collection, *By the Black Stream*), such a critical mass of artistic achievement was barely heeded in the public sphere. Now, of course, it is taken for granted, and why not? But to the teenager I then was, the very idea of there being an actual writer living a block away would have sent shivers down my back. The notion that poetry was coming from within the local community, poetry that was being received and respected and sought after by critics, editors and publishers in Britain and North America, that was very new. Even for someone such as myself who didn't really know what was going on, there was an emerging realisation that, along with the great music, dancing and social scene of Belfast clubs, poetry and fiction were starting to appear that had at their centre a groundbreaking preoccupation with the city landscape, its past and its present, which I was quite literally inhabiting, walking in and seeing but without really seeing.

My mother had bought me W.B. Yeats' *Collected Poems* for Christmas in 1970, but a couple of years earlier I had come upon Louis MacNeice's *Selected Poems*, edited by W.H. Auden, and a light of recognition went on; something about the tone of voice, the angle of mind; an ironic, restless, questioning point of view. It was MacNeice's 'English', the language that he used, which kept me going back for more, as in 'Valediction', which he wrote in his 20s:

> Cursèd be he that curses his mother. I cannot be
> Anyone else than what this land engendered me:
> In the back of my mind are snips of white, the
> sails

Of the Lough's fishing-boats, the bellropes lash
  their tails
When I would peal my thoughts, the bells pull
  free –
Memory in apostasy.

MacNeice may well have passed me by but for the
Faber Book of Modern Verse, that set text on the 'A'
Level English Literature course that I have mentioned
before on several occasions.

It was reading *The Emperor of Ice Cream* (1965),
by fellow north Belfast man Brian Moore, which struck
a chord so deep and so lasting that, in spite of all the
other wonderful novels he published, it became the
most important prompt on the way to my own writing.
When I met Brian Moore, much later on, I couldn't
help but see him as a man similar in manner, attitude
and demeanour to my own uncle, another north-
Belfast boy: stylish, self-deprecating, much travelled,
living a life elsewhere, but always, always, with Belfast
somewhere in the mix of his accent, his humour and
his concerns. Moore's slightly mid-Atlantic inflections,
his professionalism and his cosmopolitan interest in the
wider world show themselves off in the stylish realism
of his fiction and his sampling of other literature,
including the Wallace Stevens quotation for a title
(fairly hip back then), and the chat about T.S. Eliot, and
all the other alluded-to places of *The Emperor of Ice
Cream*. But there was also more immediately the inner
geography of the novel. This became a revelation. For,
having grown up with stories of the Belfast Blitz from

my grandmother and mother, and seen at first hand the impact on the landscape and the remnants of war in my own upbringing – the blackout blinds, ration books, the veterans in their military blazers, the commemorations and religious services in honour of 'the Fallen' – Moore's *The Emperor of Ice Cream* placed Gavin Burke, his young narrator, at the forefront of history, not history 'out there', over there, in Britain or Europe. No. This was history 'here', literally up the road, the Antrim Road, next door:

> He ran across the allotment, ran as fast as his legs would carry him. To the north, the guns chattered again. A new wave of bombers approached. The whole of the city seemed to be on fire. All around the night bowl of sky, from Cave Hill to the Lough, from Antrim to Down, a red glow eddied and sank, the reflected light of hundreds of burning houses, shops, factories and warehouses. Yet the streets were strangely empty. Occasionally, as Gavin half walked, half ran towards his destination, people in twos and threes would appear from some side street, glancing up at the sky as they hurried towards unknown destinations. Twice, he came upon small groups of men and women moving, dirty and dulled, among the crater ruins of their homes. People could be heard calling out the names of relatives, as though trying to

summon the dead to rise. There were few police about and, as yet, no sign of fire engines. And, always, the rumbling crash of a new explosion would drive these forlorn victims to take shelter in doorways and in other houses, sending them stumbling over broken water mains, bricks, and planks, like figures in a Biblical scene, fleeing from terrible retribution.

Elsewhere in the novel, the characters whom Gavin Burke encounters were close in many ways to the figures who attended soirées in my own grandmother's house, while all the sexual yearning and longing that Gavin experiences in the wartime city sparked off the 1960s' teenager with direct and timely coincidence.

If *The Emperor of Ice Cream* charted the coming of age of one young man at a time of great crisis (the Second World War) and his subsequent journeying to a new place of self-discovery, the sheer energy and physical passion of the music we listened to in the 1960s literally took us out of ourselves. I have written about the musical world of Belfast elsewhere, in *In Another World* (2017) and *Looking Through You* (2020). Bands such as Them had been leading the R&B charge in numerous clubs throughout the city, so when he left, with some songs in his mind, and in the States recorded the magisterial *Astral Weeks*, Van Morrison opened out a new vision of what could be done. His courage and experimenting and self-belief were, whether or not we knew it at the time, hugely liberating. Nothing could prepare you for that first listening to the mood-poem that is *Astral Weeks* and, in the decades of achievement since, Morrison has remained a singular presence.

I think we were sitting in the front room of my mother's house, or it could have been in the family apartment of a friend on the Antrim Road, or maybe downtown in Smithfield, when I first heard Morrison's dreamy, romantic, idiomatic cry of love and loss and leaving that sounded so unique and yet so recognisably of the here and now, the Belfast here and now. When he mentioned 'Sandy Row' and 'Dublin' and made those impossible rhymes rhyme in, for instance, 'Madame George', there was a shift in the earth's axis for one young man, although he would never let on, not then, not at all. As Belfast became something more of an imagined city, or maybe that should be more of a city 'imagined', other poems and novels became important to my own understanding of both the city and the different ways of writing out of it.

FIVE

I met Padraic Fiacc for the first time in the early 1970s and visited him regularly in his suburban home in Glengormley in north Belfast. He was a complicated figure who, through all the punishing years of the 'Troubles', seemed fated to carry a personal burden of guilt and anguish for what was happening in his city and elsewhere. But there was another side to Fiacc that intrigued me: the emigrant life in New York with which he was abundantly familiar, having moved there as a young boy in the 1930s, and the stories he recounted of that cosmopolitan life, based around the influx of European émigrés as much as the traditional Irish communities, were fascinating to hear, surrounded by his wife's modernistic paintings, and his references to Picasso and the great composers he listened to on the radio and played on the piano.

Fiacc looked and sounded different, and the nasal twang of his New York accent underlined his caustic, self-lacerating wit, before, that is, the curtain dropped in the mid-1970s upon his marriage and home life. In those earlier days he was as buoyant as he could be, pleased by the positive reception his first book, *By the Black Stream*, had received, including the AE Memorial Award. In *Hell's Kitchen*, one of the two programmes he wrote and narrated for BBC Northern Ireland, produced by Paul Muldoon, Fiacc's characteristic tone of voice modulates between melancholia and Belfast–New York wit:

> Here, in one school, at my most formative years, were Africa, Asia, the Middle East, and inpouring Europeans. It was exciting and scintillating, like the last glimpse of the Hudson River as we climbed the stairs down the basement entrance to report our presence to a general teacher; in our case, a Polish lady.

It certainly did not pass me by that in his first collection, *Night-Crossing* (1968), Derek Mahon, another north Belfast man, had published a poem called 'Glengormley' originally dedicated to Fiacc. And here, as with many of Fiacc's poems, the landscape of Belfast, in particular the geography of north Belfast, is rendered by the young poet with luminous detail:

> 'Wonders are many and none is more wonderful
> than man'

> Who has tamed the terrier, trimmed the hedge
> And grasped the principle of the watering can.
> Clothes-pegs litter the window ledge
> And the long ships lie in clover. Washing lines
> Shake out white linen over the chalk thanes.

The phrases which lifted off the page of those first readings still reverberate with a knowing intimacy that radiates, to quote the title of a famous novel of a little earlier, 'a kind of loving' – 'Clothes-pegs litter the window ledge' and that reference to 'washing lines'. While the more elaborate and knowledgeable mythological world is brought naturally into the frame too:

> No saint or hero,
> Landing at night from the conspiring seas,
> Brings dangerous tokens to the new era –
> Their sad names linger in the histories.

Mahon's *Night-Crossing* was brazenly at home in the world and spoke of a metropolitan excited by what he read and saw and experienced, leaving and returning to the harbour-port city that would frame his second book, the immaculate volume published in 1972 called *Lives*, with the hulk of *Titanic* rising up within scaffolding, emblazoned on the book's front cover.

It was clear then that there was an imaginative light possible from such a place of industry and almost anti-artistic endeavour; in fact, all the business was an art in itself along with the people, as in Mahon's robust poem 'Ecclesiastes':

> ... and not
> feel called upon to understand and forgive
> but only to speak with a bleak
> afflatus, and love the January rains when they
> darken the dark doors and sink hard

>into the Antrim hills, the shore, the heaped
>   graves of your fathers.

In *Lives*, Mahon came very close to home to a Protestant mindset and chaste, chastening language, a plain song of the Protestant heartlands in which I had grown up and knew, without really knowing it. Mahon had opened up the world of art and letters, writing about Edvard Munch, Samuel Beckett, Van Gogh, Cavafy, whereas in his poem 'Afterlives', from *The Snow Party* (1975), he caught how 'the hills are still the same/Grey-blue above Belfast'. I, too, had left, only to begin what Mahon calls, in his poem 'Going Home', 'a residual poetry/of leave taking and homecoming,/of work and sentiment', and had started to write my own poems with a sense of purpose, whatever about merit, and to write about poetry as well.

One of the very first books of poetry I reviewed, for the Belfast-based magazine *Fortnight*, was Michael Longley's beautiful volume *The Echo Gate* (1979). I say 'beautiful' very deliberately, because in his writing Longley has always stressed the physical, sensual pleasure of the poem. His attention to love seems to flow as a consequence of this, for instance, in the amazing tapestry of his poem 'The Linen Industry', which takes the reader on an imaginative journey from physical landscape to household to social and cultural history in the making of an embroidered flower and in love-making. There is no one else who can do this so well, this implicit mastery of image and meaning:

Since it's like a bereavement once the labour's
   done
To find ourselves last workers in a dying trade,
Let flax be our matchmaker, our undertaker,
The provider of sheets for whatever the bed –

And be shy of your breasts in the presence of
   death,
Say that you look more beautiful in linen
Wearing white petticoats, the bow on your bodice
A butterfly attending the embroidered flowers.

There was much to overshadow this revelation of a city and its history to itself, and to those coming of age in the late 1960s and 1970s and interested enough to find out what also lay side by side with the music and the poetry, there was another very different story: of the foul housing conditions, poor access to educational opportunities, a class-bound society that treated its underclass as a source of jokes. For by that time the dark shadows that had been overcast were to settle for decades throughout the North.

As a young man, busy finding a voice and working out his place in the world of the late 1960s and early 1970s, the 'Troubles' were a shattering reality check on what had been allowed to fester under the surface of Northern society: the sectarian division of a provincial society which since its inception was based upon inequality as two power blocs traded off their separate control of economic and educational opportunity and thereby sought to maintain the status quo. In his collection *North* (1979), Seamus Heaney looked squarely at what we had become, the damage done by complacent authority as much as the emotional and cultural problems of resolving imaginatively what could be done, what sway could be effected, what harm removed by the poet's voice amidst all the accusingly ugly and bloody recriminations and arguments of social division and sectarian bile.

In 'Exposure', the last poem in *North*, I found an emotional measure with which I could identify as much as argue with myself over its implications, as life away from the North was hesitant and bilocated. Like so much in Heaney's work, the poem was reassuring:

> I am neither internee nor informer;
> An inner émigré, grown long-haired
> And thoughtful; a wood-kerne
>
> Escaped from the massacre,
> Taking protective colouring
> From bole and bark, feeling
> Every wind that blows;

The 'rain' that in the opening stanza of 'Exposure' comes down through the alders, with 'its low conducive voices' muttering 'about let-downs and erosions', vividly captures the disturbance of the time, particularly the awkward, almost anti-poetical language of the 'diamond absolutes'. Poetry, Heaney suggests, is its own terrain wherein ambiguity, difference, fluidity and unpredictable things happen. Under pressure of the politics of the time – blame and the shameful acts of violence – it was hard during the mid-1970s to think beyond the immediate, which is what the penultimate name on my roll-call achieved.

Through perseverance, in the teeth of personal ill health, and with a deft tragi-comic touch, Stewart Parker's plays, particularly his masterpiece *Pentecost* (1987), resound with the civic history of Belfast. The red-brick soulscape that defined much of what the city is, even to this day, is Parker's backdrop. The industrial past, the gardens and yards, the attitudes and lifestyle, the life experience of a terraced world of side street and alleyway, the light and the shade, the urban dream within the surrounding countryside, are all heralded in Parker's drama. And in *Pentecost* he writes a great hymn to the unfolding of hope in the face of what had once been a bleak present, while circling back to love amidst war-torn Belfast during and after the Blitz and towards the present. Parker's characters live their brief stage life in the small terrace house, the setting for *Pentecost*, since it is the symbolic setting for much of Belfast city's history. Marion asks:

> So why should Lily Matthews' home and hearth be less special than Lord Castlereagh's or the Earl of Enniskillen's? A whole way of life, a whole culture, the only difference being, that this home speaks for a far greater community of experience in this country than some transplanted feeble-

minded aristocrat's ever could, have you
looked at it, properly?

It was Derry-based Jennifer Johnston, in her intensely
lyrical early novels – *The Captain and the Kings*, *The
Gates* and *How Many Miles to Babylon?* – who re-
integrated the 'Anglo-Irish' experience and the First
World War into contemporary Ireland; an achievement
all the more significant given the increasingly deadly
pressure of the Troubles throughout the 1970s so
memorably narrated in Johnston's powerful *Shadows
on Our Skin*.

Thirty years of the Troubles reached, surprisingly
enough, a stand-off between two dominant political
and religious groups. Yet the geopolitical fault lines of
the city, which Parker's *Pentecost* elegises with such
dramatic effect, are drawn even tighter today than they
were when I was growing up in the upper northside of
the city. That side of town used to be distinguished as
'mixed'. Not only did Protestants and Catholics live side
by side, but there was also a significant Jewish minority
and a varied community of sects and post-war refugees.
The cultural diversity we hear so much about these days
was a living, if unexpressed, reality in the late 1950s
and early 1960s. It died in the cut and thrust of the
early riots, and throughout the intimidation, bombing
and assassination campaigns of the 1970s and 1980s.
By the 1990s the landscape had literally changed and
the living diversity was destroyed or gone underground.

Without in any way wishing to minimise the ir-
redeemably scarred lives of those who directly suffered,

it's important to consider the net cultural impact of the 'Troubles' in Belfast. The centre-less city (grossly abused by bombers and then crassly reimagined by history-less architects) has become totally sectionalised; hollowed-out into political spheres of influence and control, with some contested and ragged remaining interfaces. While the part of Belfast where I grew up was, to some extent, integrated and civic-minded, according to findings quoted by Madeleine Leonard, there are now 'more peace lines ... located in North Belfast than in any other region in Northern Ireland and their number has increased since the first ceasefires were announced in 1994'.

The majority of children, again according to Dr Leonard, 'do not have any friends from the other religious community and a substantial number have *never* interacted socially outside their own religious grouping' (emphasis added). The contrast is stark indeed. For that neighbourhood of working-class terraces, corner shops, entries and allotments, nestled in behind lower middle-class, three-storied houses with small gardens, fronting the main roads, rising farther out towards substantial upper middle-class villas with grounds and gardens, has been undermined. Picture houses, churches, parks, bowling greens, family shops and the magical nooks and crannies, all fitted into some kind of a community living together. Not ideal, not idealised, but a living, complicated, gossipy, respectful and coherent community that could deal with itself and with private lives as well.

What I saw on a return in the early 2000s was an

ugly inversion of all that. Houses bricked-up; in one attractive triangle, which I knew like the back of my hand, the once sturdy family homes converted willy-nilly into flats; front doors with steel girders; gardens full of rubbish. Houses which I recalled standing, if sombrely, in Sunday afternoon light, blinds drawn, the outside door opened to the vestibule, were now demolished, or dark and tawdry versions of their earlier selves. Anonymous supermarkets; cheaply made-over pop-up shops, pound shops; big, windy, soulless petrol stations, derelict 1960s buildings patrolled by invisible security companies; even a spur of a motorway cutting its way right through what had once been a vibrant built-up district. Those who had lived in the inner reaches of the city had clearly fled to the suburbs or left the city for good. What I saw was the physical (psychic?) impact of political failure, sectarian head counts; a failure inscribed in the actual fabric of the place.

It is a lesson in itself when politics is driven by sectarian and not genuinely civic concerns. If such generalised pictures can ever really be believed, the fallout has taken on something of the following shape. The west of the city became 'West Belfast', a city in itself; north Belfast became a twilight zone, a lethal no man's land into which you strayed at your peril; the east withdrew further into itself, while districts, urban villages, such as Upper Ormeau, Ravenhill and Rosemount in south Belfast attempted the impossible, to hold on to as much of the shared non-sectarian Belfast codes and knowledge as was possible. It was the Canton of Hope and it survived the dark times better than most parts of the city. It is now becoming a multi-ethnic magnet and a litmus test for the Belfast of today.

The compass of Belfast has been redefined and territorialised in a radical 'decentring' of the city as a living, common civic space. The class dimensions of all this are plain to see and it may well be that the at one-time historically mixed areas will resurface in the years ahead, relocated perhaps but acting as some kind of bridgehead between the divided communities. The gated apartment blocks settling along the Lagan might show a new way forward, at least for those prosperous enough to avail of the opportunity and lifestyle. While the reclaiming and upgrading by young couples of significant parts of the older housing stock, in, for instance, the Ormeau area, could create its own kind of dynamic of renewal, provided that some sort of permanence and buoyancy is in place. On the other hand, this may well be wishful thinking. For it is not fanciful, going on what we already know, to imagine a situation in which Belfast, if current negative trends develop unchecked, will break up into culturally and/or ethnically separated entities. As the English playwright David Edgar remarked of contemporary Britain, there is a danger when 'a society narrows its self-definition to a point where substantial sections of its population are excluded ... it will end up becoming Balkanised'.

So, what should be a city with a definable hub of coherent, interrelated, expanding, outlying neighbourhoods, turns into fragmented bits of mutually antagonistic and segregated 'ghettos'; a truly shocking indictment of the political imagination post-peace process, alongside the highly financed structures for reconciliation. Yet Belfast, with its lough, hills and surrounding countryside, remains rich in possibility. One need think only of the cultural mix upon which the city was built, its maritime, commercial and industrial history, its literary, scientific and engineering achievements worldwide, to realise that human potential. Irish, Scottish, English; refugees from here, there and everywhere; religious sects, racial minorities, all with their own customs, aspirations, prejudices, ideas, experiences, desires, languages and self-understanding: all their own histories.

The main political and cultural problem facing twenty-first-century Belfast is just how the city can accommodate and foster this diversity without ending up as the cultural equivalent of a bland, second-hand modernity (such as one sees in some recent architectural redevelopment) or a sectarianism in new clothes. The violence of political and sectarian hatred has deprived the city of creating something special out of its past. It seems inconceivable to think that Belfast could remain stuck in a historical freeze-frame and languish as a capital city in a stateless limbo, one year green and the next year orange, obsessed with an irretrievable past.

Bearing in mind that a city (any city) cannot be fixed in one final version of itself, there is a critical value to be had from thinking about the kinds of continuity and crisis which made Belfast what it is: a culturally mixed city with a very mixed cultural past. Perhaps more power should be invested into Belfast and its environs so that it becomes a major regional centre, alert to its actual physical location, an arrival point between two islands and their various diverse cultures. It might be a good start if some of these blurred images and issues of authority and cultural identity were addressed honestly and clarified at a political level. To reduce this condition into a symbolic battle over flags and emblems would be further testimony only of the failure of political will to overcome the sectarian divisions of previous centuries.

SIX

The Belfast that I grew up in had much to recommend it; not that I appreciated it at the time. I can remember one key factor, which emerged during the late 1960s, just before the curtain fell. It was the fleeting growth of a renovated, energetic, non-sectarian generation which was moving into place, at ease with nationality (indeed promiscuously post-modern in that regard, well before 'hybridity' became fashionable), critically engaged by literature, politics and world events, and motivated by a sense of civil society, defiantly rejecting tribal allegiance as backward-looking. It had no singular imaginative voice, no newspaper, no critical mass, and it took no institutional form. It was critically invisible and remains a phantom. Under the weight of living through the appalling bombings and the disintegration of Belfast into localised fiefdoms under paramilitary control, this amorphous, cultural 'cement' shattered. The common civic culture, which underpinned much of Belfast, has simply eroded, like its industrial, architectural, technological and maritime past, into folk museums and heritage photography books. The younger generation probably doesn't know so much about the shadowlands of that political and cultural past life in Belfast. The nightlife and pub-life of the city is today indistinguishable from Bristol or Birmingham, or, for that matter, from Dublin's custom-built Temple Bar. We all live, more or less, in the same postmodern heaven or haven.

In his wonderful memoir, *A Country Boyhood in Belfast*, John Wilson Foster's idyll, considered against the background of the Troubles, might appear today as wishful thinking:

> When I was a boy I lived in four countries. I lived in Britain, which we called England because all our playthings were stamped 'Made in England' on their under parts. England was toy land and, at the same time, the rather stern parent from whom the toys aloofly came. Northern Ireland was not strictly a country but the place where I ran, quite literally, my heedless ways. Northern Ireland, let's say, I lived rather than lived in. In the beginning was Belfast, which in turn meant the streets of our little canton, named after Shakespearean characters whom we did not know, and so we pronounced them as we saw fit – Oberon Street, Titania Street, Glendower Street. Had we known them we might have nicknamed our canton as wits had named the Ormeau district of Palestine, Jerusalem, Cairo and Damascus streets 'The Holy Land'. But where we grew up was, in any case, 'The Holy Land'.

It may be necessary and timely to remind ourselves that this past, a very real past, was inextricably linked with the British imperial project. To deny that is to falsify the historical picture in the interests of a virtual reality; a political monoculture.

Industrialisation was at the very core of the imperial project and Belfast was a main centre of that global ambition whose religious and cultural filters meshed with empire, colossal forces (of industrialisation and the British empire) which no longer exist. Few options were made available or openly debated by the leadership of such unionist communities when change – economic, social and political – bore down relentlessly during and since the Thatcher decades. Nostalgia, in its virulent, triumphalist, as much as democratic, form, was held on to as if to a life raft. It didn't work.

In sharp contrast, the shift towards a European self-consciousness that the Republic of Ireland managed during the 1970s and 1980s, sits uneasily in Belfast precisely because of its historically intimate and highly charged emotional ties with the war-torn Britain of the 1940s and 1950s. The identification of the economic benefits that flowed (and still in large measure flow) from the British connection should also be taken into account. The North, and Belfast in particular, might have missed out on the Celtic Tiger boom years, but since the mid-1990s Belfast has been catching up. What sustained the city (and paradoxically left whole sections of the community vulnerable) was the thriving dependency culture. High rates of employment reliant upon the administration and public sector; generational unemployment; the outreach of health problems established as a way of life ('on the sick'); the emotional and moral ramifications of the victim mentality and its implications as regards local leadership and civic responsibility, have all had profound and long-lasting economic and social results.

So the battle over flags and emblems reproduces at a superficial level what carries a deeper resonance concerning the credo and iconography of the past. The countering aspects of Northern nationalism, however, appear all the more appealing to the 'outside' world of British and American groups interested in the province. This renovated Northern nationalism clearly demonstrates to the attending media a comforting and easily identifiable cultural equation: Irish equals nationalist equals Gaelic, a unified, coherent island people.

A fiction, of course, and a lasting one, in spite of all that has changed over the past two decades and more, but so unlike the endless internal rows, negativity, bickering and gracelessness associated with the fractious unionist voice, forever locked in an imperial past that the English left behind, with only the occasional nostalgic lapse, until Brexit came along and the condition became, for some, inflamed and for others, terminal. One need point only to the issue of language itself to see how the cultural weathervane has shifted. From being an underground and repressed language in twentieth-century Belfast, spoken Irish is now a dynamic and empowering mark of cultural identity for nationalists.

The revival of Irish as a spoken language throughout nationalist Belfast is truly amazing. The consciousness that culture – both upper case and lower case – is important to everyday life is intense and discussed on the airwaves and in newsprint media. But the intensity comes from 'identity' politics; not poetry. And the same is true for the 'Ulster-Scots' project, born under the sign of the Good Friday Agreement and the political equation then in fashion of 'parity of esteem'.

But what of Belfast itself? It has existed as an imagined place, more as war zone than twilight, Celtic or otherwise. One person's stereotype is another's dead certainty. As we have seen, for generations Belfast was considered in various intellectual and artistic circles as anathema to the creative spirit. Live there and perish. The shocking, unflattering images of the city in Brian Moore's novels, such as *The Feast of Lupercal* and *The Emperor of Ice Cream*, see Belfast as a desperate place, thwarting human affection, self-confidence and hope; yet the city remained unquestionably the key defining site of Moore's creative memory.

If Joyce's turn-of-the-last-century Dublin was a city of paralysis, mid-century Belfast was deadly – a cramped and dampening place, not unlike Muriel Spark's Edinburgh. To survive meant to leave and find out what the world was really like. Moore's novels from the mid-1950s can be read as his quarrel with himself and the hometown that never let him alone. Not so much as a place but as an idea, Belfast in Moore's mind means a Northern Catholic professional middle-class upbringing that haunts and taunts his writing with its religious ceremony, cultural etiquette and historical self-consciousness. Throughout his writing life, Moore deconstructed that legacy of Catholic nationalist aspiration with a cool imaginative rigour. The formal clarity of Moore's novels, the narrative compression, bright delivery of conversation, the rarity of his polished diction and the implicit moral dilemmas his novels dramatise, placed Moore at an intriguing angle to popular critical expectations about the nature and meaning of what an 'Irish writer' is, or should be. Like his accent, Moore was hard to pin down, along with the suave stylishness and urban wit, all of which strike me as peculiarly Belfast. Exile, lonely and all as it may well have been, was the making of Moore's writing. In an article published in 1974, Moore remembered leaving Belfast on a ship bound for Liverpool and a government job:

> [A] man sitting on a suitcase beside me took out a Baby Power and offered me a drink. 'Your first time across the water?' he said. 'Yes,' I said. 'What line of work are you in?' I didn't know just what I was going to do in this British government job. I had bluffed my way into it. All I knew was I was being sent abroad to some place my French would be useful. So when the man asked what line of work I was in, I began to live out my private lie. 'I'm a writer,' I said. 'Ship's writer?' he said. 'No, just a writer.' 'Would that be good wages?' 'I don't know,'

I said. Perhaps that's the way a lot of people become writers. They don't like the role they're playing and writing seems a better one.

That disarmingly anxious, self-conscious 'just a writer' has mostly disappeared today, along with the quick-witted retrieval of the last sentence, as the internationally recognised Moore looks back to the younger self voyaging out from Belfast. The sense of leaving and being uprooted is specific to Moore's own personal set of circumstances. But it carries historical reverberation even if the hundreds of thousands who currently fly in and out of Belfast's two airports carry a very different sort of baggage to that of the generation who left between the mid-1940s and the mid-1970s.

The earlier generation was following a pattern of emigration, which had become a feature of working- and middle-class life in Belfast. Attachment to the large UK-based post-war industries, at craftsman or managerial level, often meant travelling with the job. When work was not plentiful, looking for a job generally meant leaving, while the economic reasons for so doing assumed a different kind of meaning as the Troubles took root in the 1970s. Many tens of thousands decided, if they could, to relocate because of the extraordinary population shifts that were taking place as a result of the social unrest, or simply to find a 'normal' society in which to settle and rear a family. Against the backdrop of the relative stability of Belfast in the 1950s and 1960s, the provincial capital experienced some degree of prosperity. The problem was, as we all know now, that the upswing in opportunities did not percolate sufficiently throughout the various social strata of Belfast's unemployed and lower-paid workers, and the confidence to accommodate different versions of Irish identity proved either skin-deep or else withered on the vine.

The cultural straitjacket seemed all the more rigid if few of the economic benefits were widely shared. This experience of exclusion unquestionably fuelled the sense of grievance significant sections of the Catholic community felt at the denial of its legitimate political and cultural aspirations. Yet leaving was also a rite of passage, for Catholics as much as for Protestants who wanted to experience the wider, freer world beyond Belfast Lough. By the mid-1970s the matter had become rather more urgent, a choice in some instances between life and death, or between reliving the past and creating a different and possibly better future elsewhere. (In the last ten years or so the converse is true, as immigrants seek a future in Ireland.) Precious wonder then that the very fragility of self that Brian Moore's greatest novels embody is predicated upon the city he left. For Moore's characters possess a self-awareness unquestionably honed in the Belfast in which he grew up, such as how the individual deals with inordinate family pressures to conform to certain handed-down religious or political beliefs and conventions. *The Emperor of Ice Cream* is as much an examination of this moral condition in the explicitly Irish setting of Belfast as *The Statement* (1996) is in an implicitly European context. And unlike many of his contemporaries, Moore seems uninhibited when it comes to exploring the sexual life, the passionate life of his characters, men as well as women. This might have some relation to the frank, almost defiant sexuality of Belfast city life in the 1940s – from the jubilant liberating influence of the major United States Army presence to the reaction against the socially conservative and puritanical ethos of the city fathers. Moore's characters developed into sexual beings, aware of the pleasure of the body but also keenly aware of the cost of their own solitariness when rejected by, or taking an irreversible step beyond, the inherited bonds of family and home. In the intense and vigilant upbringing of his own middle-class education, Moore could not help but know how fraught the struggle was for self-understanding, when any hint of licence or criticism could be interpreted as transgression (letting down one's own 'side'); a kind of moral betrayal. The cultural configuration of such an inheritance can be viewed as distinctly Belfast-made.

SEVEN

In the opening canto of John Montague's 'The Rough Field', Belfast broods as an imposingly dangerous and dark city:

> Catching a bus at Victoria station,
> Symbol of Belfast in its iron bleakness.

The 'iron bleakness' shuts out all possible light, although, thinking back to a novel such as Sam Hanna Bell's *The Hollow Ball*, a different kind of sensual light radiates throughout the seemingly anti-sexual city where, to quote Montague's poem again, 'constraint is all'. It is the case, however, that, from eighteenth-century travellers to nineteenth-century politicians to twentieth-century writers, Belfast is bound to change in the mind's eye. Take at random examples from Patricia Craig's marvellous *The Belfast Anthology* (1999). Seeds of disaffection are recorded as well as the intimate, incoherent reasons to love the place. Here is travel writer Paul Theroux's righteous dismissal of the city in 1983:

> I had never imagined Europe could look so threadbare – such empty trains, such blackened buildings, such recent ruins:

DANGEROUS BUILDINGS – KEEP CLEAR. And bellicose religion and dirt, and poverty, and narrow-mindedness, and sneaky defiance, trickery, and murder, and little brick terraces, and drink shops, and empty stores, and barricades, and boarded windows, and starved dogs, and dirty-faced children – it looked like the past in an old picture.

Twenty years earlier, in 1962, Kate O'Brien's response is significantly deeper, even if she miscues the future – a not uncommon feature of the 1960s:

Belfast is not hard. It is not a city of brisk here-and-now: it is not spruce and forward looking; it does not roar and rush night and day towards the 1970s, the 1980s. On the contrary, its pace is easy, and it trails its immediate past and Victorian haphazardy almost too indulgently. Walking the streets alone, especially at evening, I have experienced a sharp, unlooked-for melancholy, and an inexplicable sympathy with the untidy streets and people!

Belfast, more than many other European cities, has been stereotyped to death; its complex history in permafrost; its geo-cultural life as a port, haven, hellhole, spectacle, dumbed down before the term was invented. Twenty years earlier again than Kate O'Brien's observation, the normally astute Seán O'Faolain doesn't mince words in

An Irish Journey (1940) when he comments upon the ruthlessness 'with which the whole general rash of this stinking city was permitted to spread along the waters of the Lough'. He continues:

> All the hates that blot the name of Ulster are germinated here. And what else could be germinated here but the revenges of the heart against its own brutalisation ... There is no aristocracy – no culture – no grace – no leisure worthy of the name. It all boils down to mixed grills, double whiskies, dividends, movies, and these strolling, homeless, hate-driven poor.

Caroline Blackwood's hauteur in 1973 has a similar snobbish, old-fashioned edge: 'And day after day – post-war, just as they were pre-war – in the wealthy suburbs of Belfast the wives of the industrialists went on reading the Bible, drinking sherry and eating scones.' Although, according to C.E.B. Brett in 1978, many were also having the time of their lives:

> Below the grimy and conventional surface, [Belfast] was a city bursting with a stimulating life of its own, fed by the conflicts hidden not far below the surface ... I still think that in the 1950s and 60s life in Belfast was probably more invigorating and rewarding than in Dublin, Glasgow, or any other provincial city of the British Isles.

A life which in many ways provides the subtext for the early novels of the Belfast writer Glenn Patterson, such as *Burning Your Own*, *Fat Lad* and *The International*, which take up where the fiction of Sam Hanna Bell left off. In a letter to John Boyd, Stewart Parker catches the contradictory pull when, musing on Brett's *Buildings of Belfast*, he remarks, 'Maybe people will begin to realise that there is more to the place than ugliness and bigotry – that you can love it and hate it with the same degree of intensity.' A point that Patricia Craig expands upon in her introduction to *The Belfast Anthology*:

> 'From the current policy of decimation, sweep away the whole architectural heritage of Belfast, and stick up replacements as repellent as you can make them' down to 'all kinds of enduring indigenous graces, from the city's mountainy backdrop to a special kind of urban élan, along with psychic inheritances both salutary and oppressive', you will see that Belfast is not just about 'loss' and negativity.

An interesting comparison comes to mind. Spanning the life of the old state of Northern Ireland, the poet Padraic Fiacc was born in 1924; heralding the new dispensation, Ciaran Carson was born in 1948. Both Belfast poets have imaginatively inhabited parts of the city with a truly shocking intensity that might be linked to the fact that, as Catholics, the city never quite allowed itself to be considered 'theirs' in the first place. Put at its crudest, in their work an appropriation of the city takes place that is simply not matched, or indeed attempted, by writers who come from a 'Protestant' background. 'Catholic' writers such as Padraic Fiacc or Ciaran Carson absorb everything, from the grim and ghastly to the glorious, with glee and devotion. Whatever goes on, it is a powerful imaginative ambition that we make contact with in Carson; in Fiacc, we find estranging, shocking menace. The bits and pieces of Belfast that Carson has monumentalised into song, sonnet and fiction are locally charged historical readings of place-names, streetscapes. He is like a traditional bard singing the praises and problems of his own people and their townland; it just happens to be a city called Belfast. Carson fell in love with Belfast's past and has turned the dead industrial life into a vibrant figment of his own imagination. No other writer has achieved such redemptive fidelity.

On the other hand, Fiacc, from the Markets, is the last living embodiment of the spirit of the Celtic Twilight, passed to him by Padraic Colum in New York in the 1940s, where Fiacc lived the life of an expatriate Belfast man. Profoundly Catholic, and as politically incorrect as it's possible to be, Fiacc is without doubt the greatest untold story of Irish writing. The last of the last modernists, and a name to conjure with, he was secluded in his room in a retirement home in south Belfast until his death in 2019. Fiacc's shocking travails, however, of broken-down collapse and self-mockery, are a bitter journey to the twentieth-century underworld, and the tragi-comic past of the city he lived in, off and on, for most of his ninety-five years.

It may be coincidental that one of the poems from Ciaran Carson's *The Irish for No* (1987), which took him into a new verbal and imaginative territory, should be called 'Belfast Confetti' – 'Suddenly as the riot squad moved in, it was raining exclamation marks,/Nuts, bolts, nails, car-keys'! – a phrase wryly conjured up by Fiacc in his earlier 'The British Connection', from *Odour of Blood* (1973):

> And youths with real bows and arrows
> And coppers and marbles good as bullets
> And old time thrupenny bits and stones
> Screws, bolts, nuts (Belfast confetti)

Belfast Confetti would also be the title of Carson's subsequent volume published in 1989. The anti-poetic of Fiacc's verse challenges the syntax and harmonic of 'Irish poetry' and mocks the very (Yeatsian) notion of poetry as a 'certain good'. The high oratorical ('Irish') literary past is killed off with lethal Belfast black humour. In Carson's poetry the names of things (literally anything) become the key. Is this nostalgia for the real thing?

Names map the past like ruins that haunt our present. Carson's poems strain energetically, self-mockingly, for authenticity, new points of departure between the past and present, the here and now, as he sees other cultures through the sights and sounds of his native city. The significance of Fiacc and Carson, and the many other writers, women and men, whom I haven't mentioned here, is a powerful 'local' statement of a global condition. Once a key to the industrialisation of the late nineteenth to mid-twentieth centuries, Belfast is now the imagined site upon which the end of these issues plays out. The city sits looking all ways at the same time, not unlike the mighty shipbuilding gantries of Samson and Goliath that straddle its sky, the dramatic remains of a past and far-reaching civilisation.

EIGHT

The house he had lived in was at the end of Farmley Park, a tidy suburban terrace nestled just off the main stretch of the Antrim Road, a road which connected Belfast from Carlisle Circus all the long way to Glengormley. A fine unswerving road it was, too; on a ridge between the mountains and Cave Hill and the lower Lough side, heading eventually into the Antrim countryside. Glengormley really looked like a country village. It probably felt that way, too, when Joe O'Connor and his wife, Nancy Wayne, moved there from the United States in the 1950s. When I met him there, twenty or so years later in 1973, the shadows had already closed in around his domestic life. But Joe, or Padraic Fiacc, to use his writing name, persevered with the lifestyle he had shared with poets and artists who visited him in Farmley Park, surrounded by his wife's audacious modernist paintings, the garden of birds which seemed to gather around, and the little soirées he held when he played the piano, or when, on his own, he listened to his beloved classical music, which was rarely ever off the radio. 'I wrote Sibelius and he replied but I can't find the letters,' he'd say.

Fiacc's life was chaotic, of that there is no question. Why, is another story. After he left his family home, his life went into a spiral, moving from rooming house to bedsit, until late on he found the respite, calm and stability of a residential home in which he lived for almost twenty years, revisiting his poems and receiving family and friends. He lived until his ninety-fifth year, a unique and unforgettable presence who spooked many and was loved by others; an Underground Man who probably belonged more to New York modernism than the Yeatsian romanticism he inherited from his mother. But between them both – New York and Belfast – Fiacc fashioned a poetry which is simply unrepeatable, like his life. Living on the edge, yet yearning for the very recognition he mocked, Fiacc was a man of contradictions, most certainly.

Absorbed by cruel folly and dismayed by the arrogance of the power-hungry, Fiacc always, as he said himself, was on the side of the fallen. I can still see him in his garden sweeping leaves, as he wrote in a poem, '"left over" (from the autumn)/Dead leaves, near a culvert'. Yet Fiacc's poems are full of birds – storm-birds, surely, but also birds of all kinds – jackdaws, wrens, robins, and blackbirds. Fiacc was a bird man: 'I recall yourself and the birds,' he writes in 'North Man', recounting a walk one evening along the Lagan with the writer Michael McLaverty, 'and the birds in tune with the sky gone down'. Like a medieval monk or scribe, Fiacc's eye was always drawn to the immediate sources of life, right from his earliest beginnings as a poet and throughout the often tempestuous journey of his life as a writer. Along with what he called his 'Twentieth-Century Night Life', Fiacc saw natural life as a consolation, even in the grimmest of circumstances: 'poppies/And crocuses sprout/Out of the stale dry/Dust of empty soul.' The creative pulse of making things as well as seeing things was always dear to his heart, as in the delicate balancing act of his fine poem 'Two Solitudes', which opens: 'You are baking bread./I am making a poem./We glow with silence like the full moon.'

In a telling interview, the sense of hope and optimism he felt in the family home in Glengormley in the late 1950s and early 1960s is finely captured, yet sadly overshadowed in his recollection:

> I remember two wee blackbirds getting trapped between the nylon drape and the window and fluttering madly, not able to get out; as I released them the sky darkened, a shadow came across the window just as they escaped. I'm a poet who believes in omens.

Joe's poetry is full of such moments – sudden encounters, tiny details which spring into life: 'The pruck of smoke still hovering/ Over the fry in the morning' from 'A Childhood Friend' or when he reimagines in 'Standing Water (A Rag)' the family entering into 'Nova Scotia/ Nineteen and twenty-nine, girl/Mother's delph face *creaks*, cracks ...'

It is the Northern American cold, but it is also the anxiety of the emigrant, caught between excitement, anticipation and fear:

I cling hard tight onto
A Belfast flapper's strong
Wrist bone. Her stiff new
Red leather raincoat CREAKS …

Fiacc's poetry tells us much about the struggles to succeed in the New World; a 5-year-old heading to New York. But it also, ninety years later, brings into startling focus what happens when those bad omens are not taken seriously and resolved: childhood, innocence, political violence, physical and mental struggle cross against one another and any sense of order unravels. Joe was always on the side of the less fortunate, the downtrodden, and he railed against the unacceptable conditions many ordinary people were or are forced by circumstances to endure in this or any other society.

It was of course a fluke of the purest coincidence that the day my wife and I were to be married at a civil ceremony in Belfast's City Hall, the Pope was heading to Dundalk. Consequently, as our little wedding group headed towards the Wellington Arms Hotel for the reception, bells tolled out. Belfast in 1979 had undergone a decade of violence, but, under the circumstances, we were thrilled with ourselves as family and friends from both sides of the border and from as far away as Australia gathered in the bright foyer of the hotel, then settled down for a pre-lunch drink before assembling in a side room of the restaurant set aside for the dinner party. At about 5 p.m., if memory serves me right, the second wave started to arrive – local friends at first, most of them poets.

The wine flowed, fine wine it was, too, displayed on a long, flower-bedecked trestle table. I was at the bar when I spotted Padraic Fiacc winding his way in through the large plate-glass doors. He was dressed in a tuxedo, the trousers held in place by a scarf (or was it rope?) and in his hands he was bearing a bunch of flowers, somewhat the worse for wear – both the flowers and himself. He was happy, though, and as the occasion moved up a notch or two in volume he stood up with a glass of wine in hand and repeated these words: 'God bless the Pope. I love the Pope', to which we all raised our glasses and toasted the Pontiff and Fiacc in tandem. Precisely at that moment he fell or stumbled into the trestle table and in an instant arms and hands shot out in a flurry of movement to catch the clattering bottles from hitting the floor.

My wife and I took Joe back to his Judith Hearne-like rooms in Cromwell Road; she a-glow in her spotless linen gown, me in my two-piece corduroy suit, and duly put him to bed. The evening took its own direction thereafter, as several of the guests who had travelled some distance retired to my mother's house in South Belfast where the party continued. Another poet was taken home by my then brother-in-law and myself, propped against his front door and left to the ire of what might follow as we discreetly withdrew. It was a grand night.

I repeat this story simply to make the point that my connection to Belfast's literary world, and indirectly with Padraic Fiacc, rather than being daily and regular, was social and collegial, and mostly through my visits home from Galway, where I had gone in 1974 as a 22-year-old to postgraduate study at what was then called UCG. That said, friendships were made, and while mine was a kind of associate affiliation, *The Honest Ulsterman* (*HU*) was at the centre of this relationship, alongside Blackstaff Press, which published my early poems in *Soundings*, edited by Seamus Heaney, *The Wearing of the Black*, edited by Fiacc, my first collection of poetry, *Sheltering Places*, and included in the first edition of *Poets from the North of Ireland*, edited by Frank Ormsby.

It was a heady time, and the pressures of the violence and divisions of the society really were intimate and intense. *HU* represented the local platform for poetry; it was *the* focus.

I recall sometime in the late 1970s having a heated conversation with several slightly older contemporaries in The Tavern, a famous bar in Galway's Eyre Square (no longer there, alas, amid all the grim fast-food outlets), and, in a flourish of rhetorical recognition, one of our company remarked: 'You've brought the Troubles with you!' It was a reminder of just how fraught life would become by the time of the hunger strikes in 1981.

HU mocked and satirised its way through how these tensions were often portrayed and was unbowing (wisely I think today) to similar pressures of a much more immediate and pressing kind. Back then many were trying to understand what could be done to respond in some meaningful way to what was happening. But I see now, all these years later, that those of my age who had grown up in the 1960s in Belfast were actually in shock; a kind of stunned disbelief that what was going on was actually going on, since we had lived our teenage years free from the poison of sectarianism.

Padraic Fiacc became the voice of that shock and disbelief, but his aesthetic of violence, ripping up the sonorities and structure of poetry in an effort to register his profound disquiet, underwent a cruel intensifying pressure when Gerard McLoughlin, one of the young lads who, trying to write poems, were drawn to him, was assassinated.

Fiacc's marriage had collapsed and now the abominable killing seemed to pitch him over the edge. His poems, along with several public statements, revealed the disturbed psychic condition of his life during the 1970s and 1980s. His anarchic and crazy irreverence, a lethal urban form of dispossession, was matched by a deeply held reverence for religious rites, omens of one kind or another, and a subversive, confessional nature that riled the political purists on all sides.

If *HU*'s 'position' was to maintain the integrity of poetry and the belief that a poet should not succumb to 'the latest outrage', Fiacc's poetry (and to a certain extent, his own self) became a rejected figure; a position he was both attracted to and played upon, as 'anti-establishment', an outsider. And yet this wasn't really the case.

From the 1980s Fiacc received recognition: his poetry had a readership, and his own personal and literary history, from his emigrant life in pre-Second World War New York to his return to pre-Troubles Belfast in the 1950s, had found resonance in wider society. There was the relative success of his writing, too, including the early awarding of the prestigious AE Memorial Award; the publication by The Dolmen Press of *By the Black Stream*, his first collection, in 1969; regular contributions to numerous Irish broadsheets and literary journals; broadcasts on national radio; and inclusion in poetry anthologies such as James Simmons' *Ten Irish Poets*. He also found space in *HU*, as well as being the subject of parodies of his style and demeanour. Fiacc became known briefly as 'The Man Most Touched'. But he gave as good as he got. And there were the two BBC Northern Ireland programmes – *Hell's Kitchen* and *Atlantic Crossing* – produced by Paul Muldoon, which are well worth listening back to or reading in *My Twentieth-Century Night-Life*, edited by Patrick Ramsey and published by Lagan Press, which also published *Ruined Pages*, the standard edition of Fiacc's selected poems. To say nothing of his becoming part of Muldoon's roll-call in 'Incantata':

> Of Marlborough Park, of Notting Hill, of the Fitzroy Avenue
> immortalized by Van 'His real name's Ivan' Morrison, 'and him the dead spit
> of Padraic Fiacc', of John Hewitt, the famous expat,
> in whose memory they offer every year six of their best milch cows,
> of the Bard of Ballymacarrett,
> of every ungodly poet in his or her godly garret,
> of Medhbh and Michael and Frank and Ciaran and 'wee' John Qughes.

It was Muldoon, also, who described Fiacc – the counter-spirit to *HU* and its aesthetic – as a figure representative 'of the condition of being a poet that many, including me, shy away from. I admire Fiacc for that and for what he's done and what he represents', which seems like a fair estimation to my way of thinking. Padraic Fiacc's quixotic presence is becoming increasingly understood as part of the history of Northern Irish writing. As I previously remarked, I met and knew Fiacc from 1973 – to be exact – and during the 1970s we visited him regularly in Glengormley. He also ventured forth to Galway, most memorably in 1976 to attend and give a reading at the Second International IASAIL (as it then was) Conference in UCG (now NUIG). That is a story all to itself and best left for another time.

By the mid-1980s I was seeing less of him, until my friend Aodán Mac Póilin (a key Fiacc benefactor and supporter, along with his wife, Áine Andrews, and their daughter, Aoife) and I decided to edit a new and updated edition of Joe's poems, since Terence Brown's important edition of 1979 was no longer in print. We spent quite some time getting this work together and in order for Blackstaff Press, which published *Ruined Pages* in 1994. It was an extraordinary few years leading up to the publication and, thanks to several local supporters and friends, and to the photographer John Minihan (who got Joe out and about again), his drift into a kind of dangerous itinerant existence, moving from rooming house to rooming house, was resolved. Finally, he would settle in the secure and compassionate environment of a residential care home in south Belfast in the 1990s.

The task of chaperoning Joe to give an interview on BBC Radio Ulster to a sedate but sympathetic interviewer was certainly 'an experience'. Prior to the interview taking place – a torturously stop-start affair of silences and stutters filled by my efforts at connecting the dots at the interviewer's imploring nods – we sat in the hospitality room drinking coffee. We were joined shortly afterwards by a well-known singing duo of the time who were promoting their tour as their 'hit' was being played widely on the airwaves. Not that Joe would have known this, of course. The couple, a man and a woman, sat down with us and, under Joe's beady eye, the gold bracelets and rings and fashionable clothes of the performers drew a remark in typical mid-Atlantic accent: 'Are yous Mafia?' followed by the rasping high laugh. They didn't know what to make of it all, nor, alas, did the goodly interviewer.

By the time I had Joe bundled into a taxi and returned him to Wellesley Avenue, the telephone exchange at BBC HQ was buzzing with complaints about 'this poet' and his manner, views which followed Fiacc wherever he went and led to his rebellious anti-hero reputation. The truth of his life was rarely, if ever, touched upon, or the anarchic, satiric energy he embodied in his unique view of things, such a telling part of the Belfast he identified with, at odds with the official versions of the city provided by varying political agendas and their expected manners and decorum.

Joe could be infuriatingly (and wearyingly) dis-ruptive and, at his worst, destructive. But that was only an element of the personality, inflamed by distress and disappointment, along with sexual confusions and the legacy of his vulnerable mental health. There was an emotional delicacy and care that the poems reveal, and a wicked sense of fun, too – urbane, rascally New York–Belfast wit, one-liners which could bring the house down. There was a touch of the genius buried within the self-pity and the recklessness.

Once, when our rendezvous in Galway went astray, he called into the local convent where my partner was teaching in the early 1970s and, having met the Mother Superior, joined the rest of the nuns for tea and biscuits. Later in the week Joe gave a reading at the school's request to a spellbound assembly hall full of Leaving Certificate students. He could produce such moments of simple yet sublime calmness and intensity without frightening or alienating his audience.

There is no one like Fiacc. No one else could or should follow in his tempestuous and alarming footsteps along the abyss, but at long last it looks like the reality of his life and the meaning of his work are coming increasingly into critical alignment.

As John Minihan has remarked, Fiacc reminds him of the artist Francis Bacon, and in Minihan's portraits of Bacon, William Burroughs and Samuel Beckett, he has produced his own canon of artistic excellence to which can be added, without any special pleading or distortion, Padraic Fiacc. An outsider, most certainly, but one whose life was inseparable from his passionate, disputable art, Fiacc is a poet who belongs equally in the company and wider frame of European modernism as much as being read as the chronicler of the shocking local history of the Northern conflict and its sectarian savagery.

In one of his best-known and best-loved poems, 'First Movement', the presentiments and omens of nature are embedded in the local inner-city Belfast landscape which Fiacc opens up outwards; a simple, but to my mind simply wonderful, poem, carrying within itself the sources of vision which Joe's poetry always searched for, even during the worst of his times when he lived so desperately close to the jagged edges of our unimaginable troubles.

> Low clouds, yellow in a mist wind,
> Sift on far-off Ards,
> Drift hazily ...
>
> I was born on such a morning
> Smelling of the Bone Yards
>
> The smoking chimneys over the slate roof tops
> The wayward storm birds
>
> And to the east where morning is, the sea
> And to the west where evening is, the sea
>
> Threatening with danger
>
> And it would always darken suddenly.

Fortunately, Fiacc was to reclaim and experience calm in the last couple of decades of his life. 'Alive Alive

O' – which conveys his mischievous and irreverent spirit while touching upon his presence as the irascible outsider he could not help himself from being – catches the spirit that lives on in the poems he spent a lifetime in making:

> The altar boy from a Mass for the dead
> Romps through the streets of the town
> Lolls on brick-studded grass
> Jumps up, bolts back down
> With wild pup eyes …
>
> This morning at twist of winter to spring
> Small hands clutched a big brass cross
> Followed the stern brow of the priest
> Encircle the man in the box …
>
> A bell-tossed head sneezed
> In a blue daze of incense on
> Snivelled bit lips, then
> Just to stay awake, prayed
> Too loud for the man to be at rest …
>
> O now where has he got to
> But climbed an apple tree!

In his memory, and in memory, too, of a troubled time which will be associated in my mind with Joe O'Connor/ Padraic Fiacc, I wrote this brief elegy:

Leaves for Burning
for Padraic Fiacc, 1924–2019

Are you spinning in your grave yet?
More than likely you've found a perch
among the noisy blackbirds on a sparse
tree where you can snipe from branch
to branch, settle yourself and spot
what else is going on, hither and yon.

The boys who went down in the dark,
the fine old lady everyone knew,
and loitering there, amidst the Celtic crosses,
someone's draining a can as the sky sweeps
up high into the black mountain
and down the other side to your garden.
Look just now, dead leaves for burning,
and it's before all over again.

NINE

I am a product of the way war casts people together – as civilians in a time of war, as men and women in the armed forces – as much as it hurls people against each other in acts of barbarity, no matter how we weigh the morality of cause. Simply put, my late mother was a keen admirer of all kinds of music in performance. As a very young woman she fell in love with my musician-father. Originally from a family from the Welsh–English border, he was London-born and joined the Royal Inniskilling Fusiliers band at a young age. The band toured Northern Ireland for a morale-boosting celebration towards the end of the Second World War. They were married in 1945. The marriage lasted until the mid-1950s, whereupon my sister and I and my mother relocated to my grandmother's house in north Belfast. It was during this time – the mid- to late 1950s – that the aftermath of the war registered with me.

For 'the war' – the Second World War was colloquially known as simply 'the war' – was literally everywhere. Barely a decade had gone by since its end, and Belfast was still very much marked by the experience. The physical landscape bore the scars of the deadly blitz of 1941 – when almost 1,000 citizens had perished – and in the quasi-industrial pop-up camps that had been created to house army installations, garages, depots and the like, one could still wander. As young boys we did so, picking up the habits of bubble-gum, hairstyle and, latterly, dance moves from the long-departed American troops who had been stationed nearby. The 'prefabs' – as temporary housing was called – remained along north Belfast's Shore Road. But the sense of a ceremonial life in honour of those who had lost family members during the war was very much an accepted and unselfconscious part of our upbringing in school and in social and civic life. More intimately, the house in which I spent my early years retained fixtures of the war – blackout blinds to seal off any light that might benefit Luftwaffe bombers remained in place on the bedroom windows upstairs; ration-books were left in a kitchen press, and the language and customs that were associated with rationing carried over well into the 1950s. Food was not thrown out; clothes were repaired, socks darned and these practices continued not out of thrift but out of habit. The human dimension of this post-war world retains a very special resonance for me, bearing in mind what would descend upon the city of Belfast by the end of the 1960s.

In the house I moved to in the mid-1950s, with its random relics of wartime, I took in, without actually knowing it, many stories of precisely how war recasts what seems to be the stabilities and securities of 'home'. My mother and her brother were evacuated after the first blitz in Belfast to the Antrim countryside from their own family home to which they had returned from Canada in the mid-1930s. It was in this house in north Belfast that refugees, contacts of friends of my grandmother, had briefly passed through on their way to Canada. I was fascinated to hear about the CID calling to that house to interview my grandmother about one such friend, one of the fleeing émigrés, only to be confronted by *her* straight-laced and stalwart father, who denied any such knowledge and sent the police on their way. Or so the story goes.

Around that house and the surrounding avenues and terraces off the Antrim and Cliftonville roads, the Nazi bombs would fall and create carnage in the blitz of 1941. If the aftermath of war had left its mark on the streetscapes of Belfast, one can also see in retrospect how lives had been not so much 'influenced' by the war as determined by it. Men in their regimental blazers heading to the British Legion sporting pencil-thin moustaches, raincoats folded neatly over arm, turned out well was the phrase. One of our neighbours, who never fully recovered from the experience of being torpedoed, could be heard crying out at night for his friend and second-in-command whom he had lost at sea. The strained understanding of their women was stretched, no doubt, to breaking point. A friend's father, who had been a rear gunner on a Lancaster (a perilous position with high mortalities), never referred to his war experiences and would unaccountably turn morose and barely talk for days on end.

A neighbour, literally next door, a quiet unassuming civil servant who had fought with the British Army through the bitter campaigns liberating Europe, found himself finally in Vienna, where he met and married

Elsa, with whom he returned to Belfast to live a subdued life before illness struck him down in middle-age. Elsa seemed so foreign in manner and style and custom. One evening my mother, to whom she was very close, recounted the truth of Elsa's hounded wartime existence, dressed as a man to avoid rape when the avenging Soviet troops settled their grim score with the Third Reich. There were other such stories which I heard without quite understanding. I had another friend whose mother was Czech. She was a wonderful, quietly mannered and sophisticated woman, but who amongst us could know what she had gone through, of what had happened that took her across Europe to a suburban home in north Belfast. Our boyhood was peopled with many such stories.

The anecdotes I eagerly listened to when 'soirées' gathered in our house included recollections about the Pathé newsreels that featured the release from the camps of desperate, unbelievable figures. Those who watched laughed at first and thought that what they were seeing on the screen was a 'horror' movie until the reality dawned that this was actual. My mother recounted how people in the Capitol cinema on the Antrim Road fainted or were sick and fled. When I started at the Lyric Youth theatre as a young, impressionable teenager, our dance instructress was a wonderful woman called Helen Lewis, who had been incarcerated in a concentration camp (her camp number was stamped on her arm) – experiences which she recounted in *A Time to Speak*, one of the few Holocaust survivor accounts from Ireland.

As a British city, as Belfast so publicly and officially was then, in a way it can no longer be, the airwaves were awash with military ceremonials and commemorations. Victory and the world at war, and the history of the war in Europe, was part and parcel of our education, our schoolbooks, our calendar, our church, our scout 'troop'. The abomination of the Holocaust and the oppressions that befell Europe during the war, and after, with the cruelty of the Iron Curtain and the displacement of millions of people throughout Europe, concentrated the legacy of the Second World War on our Britishness – the military tattoos come summer, the quasi-military role-playing of the Boys Brigade, and in the pervasive expectation of being 'in the right' since 'we' had 'won' after all.

As I have noted earlier, British history, in particular the social and cultural aftermath of the Second World War, was a defining feature of my generation. As far as 'Europe' was concerned, it was a Europe in fundamental ways distant, even though, ironically, it was quite liter-ally next door. It started to take on a much more per-sonal meaning, like most things, as I grew slightly older.

I started to read through the magnificent Penguin European Poets series that appeared in the mid- to late 1960s, poets who were not on any 'reading list' at school or college, particularly the Russian poet Anna Akhmatova. Other poets from former Eastern European countries, such as Vasko Popa from Yugoslavia, became increasingly read and more available in English translation, bringing with them a much wider sense of the experience of war in Europe.

Here Ted Hughes, one of the most important pro-
ponents of this trans-European writing, makes the case
for its centrality:

> I think it was [Czeslaw] Milosz, the Polish
> poet, who when he lay in a doorway and
> watched the bullets lifting the cobbles out
> of the street beside him realised that most
> poetry is not equipped for life in a world
> where people actually do die. But some is
> … In a way, their world reminds one of
> Beckett's world.

The reference to Milosz is pertinent (not to mention
Beckett), because around the same time as the European
poets of the post-war were finding an audience in
translation, Milosz was himself being translated, or
re-translated, into English. *The Captive Mind*, his
classic study of war, its bloody aftermath in Soviet
totalitarianism, originally published in English in 1953,
was reissued by Penguin in 1980 and found a deep
echo in literary circles on both sides of the Atlantic,
probably because Milosz was writing out of and in
turn addressing the politically fraught and dangerous
immediacies of the Cold War, the first serious cracks of
which were beginning to show.

So to the young poet reading this material in the
late 1960s and 1970s, the sense of war, of the Second
World War, of history being made or remembered,
there was a strong complicating sense of identification
with the places and poetry of Europe – Prague, Paris,

Warsaw, Leningrad. Names that had once been only that, 'names' on a map, took on an actual life of their own, like London or Belfast; places known, lived in, familiar. The local world I knew, though entering its own crisis of political violence in the late 1960s, early 1970s, had common bonds, parallels and comparisons both historically with the aftermath of the Second World War and *culturally* in the opening up of non-English-language poets whose work was now relatively easy to collect in the Belfast bookshops of the time. I wrote poems clearly straining to the example of the great European figures. By the time my second book of poems appeared in 1985, there was a more coherent sense that 'Europe' was not so much a 'concept' or 'idea' as a way of life and writing; of seeing things. In a literary sense, Michael Longley and Derek Mahon, and before them MacNeice, had shown the way. It took me another ten years – discovering, working and travelling through various European and former East European countries – to understand; to *see* what had happened.

In *The Morning Train* (1999), which collected poems from those journeys of the previous decade or so, that experience crystallised around a group of poems – 'The Minos Hotel', 'Europa', 'The Old Jewish Cemetery, Lodz', 'The Night's Takings' and 'In Ron's Place'. The last-named poem starts off in the much-loved, much lived-in home from home of a friend's outside Lucca in Tuscany. While recovering from an ailment, I could hear conversations on the little roof garden overhead and I drifted off. For some reason a train journey across the middle of Slovakia came to mind. It had been quite a trip overnight and midway through that journey the thought had struck me about all the other train journeys that had taken place on similar rail networks to those we had been using. It was a scarifying feeling – the ordinary day life of a harmless journey on what had once been nightmarish terminals barely thirty or forty years before. 'In Ron's Place' celebrates the respite and pleasures of (our temporary) home with the haunted and haunting landscape of another time, another place:

> I was sitting up in Ron's place
> among the mountains,
> church bells followed by church bells,
> then 'April in Paris',
>
> when I realized that a person
> can only take so much in.
> I'd been lying in my cot
> for the guts of a week –
>
> Hong Kong or Singapore flu –
> and could hardly lift my head for you,
> lover, lady, wife.
> I thought this was it –
>
> the end, to simply waste away,
> *neutral and inert*,
> without a bit taken,
> the brassy taste of stomach juices,

swollen glands, blocked passageways,
the shivers, energy levels
at an all-time low,
when, as I say,

I was listening to Bird, 'April in Paris',
the church bells went counting,
then the tower up here
in the silent hills,

where the only sound
is the postman's moped,
a couple of voices under the window,
before you really see

the mountains beneath us
and the brazen light of day
over all things, great and small –
lizards slipping in and out

of the warming roof tiles,
the logs dissembling into cobwebs
and dust, the table and chair
moved to where you take the sun …

And I fall back to sleep,
this time in a couchette,
listening to the wheels brace and tack
to miles and miles of railway track.

At one station –
its long name in black and white,
the row of lorries parked in
a yellowish light from the waiting room –

the deadpan voice announces
where we are and where we are going next
as we arrive and depart
the all-night factories, the cubist blocks

of flats, the shapes of installations
in the darkness, snowy embankments,
sidings, cranes, sheds,
and then nothing again.

The countryside flees
and I wake with a jolt.
Are you still there?
Is the sun still out?

ENDNOTE

In the autumn of 1974, as a 22-year-old, I took the Ulsterbus to Monaghan town, and from there boarded the CIÉ coach that wound its way through several counties before arriving at Éamonn Ceannt Station off Eyre Square in Galway. It was almost fifty years ago. The Belfast I had left behind no longer exists, except in people's minds and memories. The republic I was travelling through has also been transformed, including the somewhat sleepy market town that was Galway. How can one ever remember the tone and timbre of the 1970s and the values of the Republic that really were on the cusp of lasting change? It was a different world, for sure, but some things remain lodged in the memory of that time. Like the grotesque disfiguring violence inflicted upon ordinary people by the paramilitaries and various units of the British Army; like the long and arduous battle women of all classes and backgrounds had to endure to achieve basic civil liberties in their own country; like the demeaning deference expected by a male-possessed Church and the preening patronising of many (male) politicians.

But I also have a lasting sense of the edgy, challenging focus of the culture that was calmly self-confident and productive of counter-images and contrary views. I have no nostalgia for that time, although thinking about my life in the west of Ireland in the 1970s and 1980s sounds again like a 'sheltering place' from the travails and troubles of the Belfast I had in part left behind during those years in Galway's old city, around the streets and canal-ways, the bridges, lough shore and harbour where we used to live.

It is hard to think of how things could have been so different without making it seem as if things turned out not as well as one had hoped, which is not the case. The fact is, though, that no one back then that I knew really planned a future. It just happened. Maybe that is the biggest change I can spot between then and now. Targets, outcomes, graphs and statistics, the numerical volumes to which we seem to be increasingly addicted in post-Celtic Tiger, twenty-first-century Ireland, forecasting everything from weather to economic predictions to just about every facet of social life. These strainings after certainty certainly did not exist in the years covered by this memoir. We lived more in the moment. That may have been unwise, I don't know, but what I can say is that the not-knowing about these matters did not halt our growth or stunt our enthusiasm for life.

The petulance, complaint and unceasing quest for factoids and percentages, faults and failings, blame and admonishment which characterise so much of Irish life today, and its anxiety-inducing, and, at times, bullying social media, did not play any part in our life back then, or if it did it hasn't left any trace behind in my memory. Politics was cut and thrust; business was precisely that, business: nothing more, nothing less but nothing like the current fad for elevating it to a new religion.

There was an intelligent debate going on about, among many other things, literature and art that were not in hock to the marketplace, the mantra of tourist economics or the virtue-signalling egotism and narcissism which fills up vast swathes of the digital and media world. Perhaps surprisingly, too, there was an openness and appetite in brashly engaging with European ideals, probably because we had only recently joined the European family. This act would prove critical in underpinning the modernisation of infrastructure in Ireland, north and south, and the liberalisation of our codes of conduct. But also, critically, the opening of our minds as well; no longer being obsessed with England, for one thing, started to take root sometime around the 1970s.

While the missing women's voices witnessed in these pages have been transformed in the decades which follow the closing of my particular chapters, I thought it would be less than honest to rewrite, with present-day beliefs and expectations in mind, the history as I had lived it, as it happened. I hope the volumes which make up *Northern Chronicles* (*Another World, Looking Through You,* concluding with *A City Imagined*) sort some of the historical bass notes into a record of personal time. From growing up in a vibrant 1960s' Belfast, through the blunt decades that at times followed, before the Republic soared economically and then crashed unceremoniously, leaving the ordinary 'Joe' to pick up the tab. And now what? This book ends with more questions than it can possibly answer. Who knows what the future brings? Certainly not the young lad I remember disembarking from the dewy CIÉ coach one crisp late afternoon off Eyre Square in Galway, many moons ago.

ACKNOWLEDGEMENTS

A City Imagined: Belfast Soulscapes draws upon contributions to programmes broadcast on RTÉ Radio One, Lyric FM and BBC Northern Ireland. Some sections were originally published in different versions in *The Rest is History* (1998), *The Cities of Belfast*, edited by Nicholas Allen and Aaron Kelly (2003), *Catching the Light* (2007), *Irish Culture and Wartime Europe*, edited by Dorothea Depner and Guy Woodward (2013), *The Stoic Man* (2015), and in *The Irish Times*, *Irish Pages*, *Fortnight* and *Reading Ireland*, to whose editors kind acknowledgement is made and, also, to Peter Fallon and The Gallery Press for permission to quote from Gerald Dawe's poetry.

For his support and vigilant editorial eye, my thanks and appreciation to the peerless Jonathan Williams, and my deepest thanks also to Conor Graham, publisher at Merrion Press, for bringing the three volumes of *Northern Chronicles* to a safe landing with the publication of this book. It has been a real privilege to work with him and all the team in Newbridge, County Kildare.

SELECT READING

Craig, Patricia, *The Belfast Anthology* (Belfast: The Blackstaff Press, 1999).

— *Brian Moore: A Biography* (London: Bloomsbury, 2002).

Dawe, Gerald, *The Morning Train* (Oldcastle: The Gallery Press, 1999).

— *The Last Peacock* (Oldcastle: The Gallery Press, 2019).

Fiacc, Padraic, *Ruined Pages: New Selected Poems* (Belfast/Derry: Lagan Press, 2012).

— *My Twentieth-Century Night-Life: A Padraic Fiacc Miscellany* (Belfast: Lagan Press, 2009).

Foster, John Wilson, 'A Country Boyhood in Belfast', *Irish Literary Supplement*, Vol. 8, No. 2, 1 September 1989, pp. 12–13.

Heaney, Seamus, *North* (London: Faber and Faber, 1975).

Johnston, Jennifer, *The Captain and the Kings* (London: Hamilton, 1972).

— *The Gates* (London: Hamilton, 1973).

— *How Many Miles to Babylon?* (London: Hamilton, 1974).

— *Shadows on Our Skin* (London: Hamilton, 1977).

Leonard, Madeleine, 'Sectarian Childhoods in North Belfast', in *Uncertain Ireland: A Sociological Chronicle 2003–2004*, edited by Mary P. Corcoran and Michel Peillon (Dublin: Institute of Public Administration, 2006).

Lewis, Helen, *A Time to Speak* (Belfast: Blackstaff Press, 1992).

SELECT READING

Longley, Michael, *The Echo Gate* (London: Secker and Warburg, 1979).

MacNeice, Louis, *Collected Poems* (London: Faber and Faber, 2007).

Mahon, Derek, *Night-Crossing* (London: Oxford University Press, 1968).

— *Lives* (London: Oxford University Press, 1972).

Montague, John, *New Collected Poems* (Oldcastle: The Gallery Press, 2012).

Moore, Brian, *The Emperor of Ice Cream* (London: André Deutsch, 1965).

Muldoon, Paul, *The Annals of Chile* (London: Faber and Faber, 1994).